HARRY S TRUMAN
1884 -

Chronology-Documents-Bibliographical Aids

Edited by

HOWARD B. FURER

Series Editor

HOWARD F. BREMER

1970

OCEANA PUBLICATIONS, INC.

Dobbs Ferry, New York

Library of Congress Catalog Card Number: 75-83749
Standard Book Number: 379-12067-4

Manufactured in the United States of America

CONTENTS

EDITOR'S FOREWORD

Every attempt has been made to cite the most accurate dates in this Chronology. Memoirs, diaries, documents, newspapers, and similar evidence have been used to determine the exact date. However, some of the events cited have been given conflicting dates in several of the sources used. In such cases, the most plausible date has been listed. Should this Chronology be in conflict with other authorities, the student is urged to go back to the original sources, as well as to the Truman *Memoirs,* and the *Encyclopedia of American History* edited by Richard B. Morris.

The aim of this volume is to provide in a single handy book the essential historical facts about the life, and especially, the administrations of Harry S Truman. While it does make some judgments on the significance of events, it is hoped that they are reasoned ones based on an understanding of the subject and the period of history during which he lived.

Obviously, much more could have been included in this book, but space limitations forced the writer to be selective in his choice of pertinent facts, key documents, and a critical bibliography. This research tool, however, provides an excellent starting point for the interested student who can then investigate for himself additional and, or, contradictory materials. The documents in this volume are taken from: Government Printing Office, *The Public Papers of the Presidents: Harry S Truman, 1945-1953.* 8 vols. Washington, D.C. 1961-1967.

CHRONOLOGY

YOUTH, WORLD WAR I, AND BUSINESS LIFE.

1884

May 8   Born: Lamar, Missouri as Harry S Truman. Father: John Anderson; Mother: Martha Ellen Young.

1885

May 1   Family moved to Cass County, Missouri, south of Harrisonville, where Truman's father ran a farm.

1886

April 25   Brother, Vivian, born.

1887

March   Family moved again to the Sol Young farm at Grandview in Jackson County. Sol Young was Harry's maternal grandfather.

1889

August 12 Sister, Mary Jane, born on the Young farm.

1890

December 12 Family moved to Independence, Missouri, where Harry's father bought a large house. He also operated a farm southeast of town, and went into buying and selling of livestock.

1892

September 1 Began his education at the Noland School in Independence, continued at the Columbian School, and graduated from Independence Central High School in June, 1901. During his high school days, young Harry worked at Clinton's Drugstore. He was a good student, especially fond of history, and learned to play the piano.

1901

September   Harry's father, having financial difficulties at this time, was unable to send him to college, while poor eyesight

1

kept Truman from receiving an appointment at both West
Point and Annapolis.

September 15 Took a temporary job as a timekeeper with the Santa Fe
Railroad.

1902

August 10 Went to work in the mailing room of the Kansas City *Star*
at $7 a week.

October Family now moved to Kansas City, where Truman decided
he wanted to be a banker. Worked for the National Bank of
Commerce, and then, for the Union National Bank.

1904

July 21 Family moved back to Grandview, but Truman stayed on in
Kansas City living in a boarding house.

1905

February 16 Joined Battery B of the National Guard of Kansas City
at the rank of private.

1906

January Left his job at the Union National Bank and went back to
the farm at Grandview, where he worked until 1917.

1909

February 9 Received his first degree in the Masonic Order, Belton
Lodge No. 450 at Belton, Missouri.

March 9 Received his third degree in the Masonic Order. His
membership in the Masons later helped his political career.

1914

November 5 Father, John Anderson, died. Harry was at his bedside.
Father's death made Harry man of the house.

November 15 For sentimental reasons, Judge Robert Mize of the Eastern
District of Jackson County, gave Truman his father's old
post as road overseer of Washington Township. When
Harry proposed an ambitious road-overhaul program, he
provoked an argument, and lost his job.

1915

April 1 Congressman William P. Boland named Truman post-
master of Grandview at $50 a month. Truman gave the

money to his assistant. Began attending meetings of the Kansas City Tenth Ward Democratic Club headed by Michael Pendergast, the brother of Thomas Pendergast, the political boss of Kansas City and its environs.

1916

September 25 Invested $5,000 in the Atlas-Okla Oil Lands Syndicate, and became treasurer of this new firm. The entry of the United States into World War I, put an end to the company's activities.

1917

April 6 United States declared war on Germany.

May 22 Truman elected a first lieutenant of Battery F of the second Missouri Field Artillery.

August 5 Truman and his state unit sworn into the federal service, the unit becoming the 129th Field Artillery of the 35th Division.

September 26 Truman's artillery unit entrained for Camp Doniphan at Fort Sill, Oklahoma for combat training.

1918

March 20 Truman left Camp Doniphan for Rosedale, Kansas, after having been chosen for promotion and the Overseas School Detail.

March 30 Sailed from New York City for France on the troopship *George Washington.*

April 13 Arrived at Brest, and was sent to the Second Corps Field Artillery School at Montigny-sur-Aube.

July 4 Sent to Angers for more training at one of Napoleon's old artillery camps, Coëtquidan.

July 11 Put in command of Battery D of the 129th Field Artillery unit.

September 6 Saw first action against the enemy in the Vosges Mountains.

**September
12-16**   Truman's unit moved to the St. Mihiel campaign, where it occupied positions on the 35th Division's front for the Meuse-Argonne drive.

**September
26-29**   Distinguished himself in the fighting along the Meuse-Argonne line.

October 10   Informed by letter that he had been promoted to the rank of Captain. The promotion had actually been in effect since the preceding May.

October 27   Commanded his battery in support of the 35th and 1st Divisions in front of Verdun in the Sommedieu sector.

November 6   Participated in the fighting at Metz.

November 11 At eleven o'clock, the armistice was signed, ending the war.

**December
7-10**   Went to Paris on leave with several other officers. Visited Nice and Monte Carlo as well. Was not impressed with behavior of French society.

1919

April 9   Embarked from Brest for the United States on the German passenger liner *Zeppelin*.

April 20   Arrived in New York on Easter Sunday morning. Truman had been overseas for one year and twenty days.

May 6   Discharged from the army at Camp Funsten, Kansas. When he returned to civilian life, Truman was thirty-five years old.

June 28   Truman and Elizabeth (Bess) Virginia Wallace, a childhood sweetheart, were married at Trinity Episcopal Church in Independence, Missouri.

November 29 With his partner, Eddie Jacobson, Truman opened a haberdashery store in Kansas City. He invested $15,000 in the store, the money having been raised from the sale of equipment and stock from the Grandview farm.

1921

January 1   The store did well during its first two years in operation. As of this date, Truman and Jacobson had a $35,000 inventory at cost.

1922

January 1   By this time, the post-war boom gave way to a post-war depression, and the store's inventory had shrunk to $10,000. Creditors and banks began to press Truman and Jacobson.

April 21   Hopelessly in debt, Truman and Jacobson closed their store, but did not declare bankruptcy. Truman determined to pay all of his debts. Although Jacobson finally declared bankruptcy in February, 1925, Truman continued to pay his creditors until the mid-1930's when the long years of financial misery finally came to an end.

POLITICAL CAREER

1922

August 1   Encouraged by the Kansas City political organization of Thomas J. Pendergast, Truman turned to politics. He won a four sided race in the Democratic primary for the nomination for Judge of the County Court of the Eastern District of Jackson County.

November 4   Truman defeated Republican opponent for the office of County Judge by a huge majority.

1923

January 15   Truman sworn into office. Despite the heavy financial burdens of the county, and Pendergast machine rule, Truman was a very active judge, fostering many improvements, especially in road construction.

September 18   Enrolled in Kansas City Law School for evening classes. Truman attended the academic years of 1923-24 and 1924-25, but was forced to drop out because of personal reasons.

1924

February 17   Daughter, Mary Margaret, born in Kansas City.

November 6   Ran for reelection as eastern judge, but was defeated by a harness maker, Henry Rummel by 876 votes. This was the only defeat ever suffered by Truman in an election.

1925

January 7   Out of work again, Truman took a job with the Automobile Club of Kansas City, where he remained for about a year and a half. Earned an excellent salary.

1926

November 2   Ran for office of Presiding Judge of Jackson County, and with the aid of the Pendergast machine, was elected by a margin of 16,000 votes. Throughout the campaign, he had promised to provide honest, economic government.

1928

May 4   Judge Truman's bond issue for improved roads, hospitals and courthouses was carried by a three-fourth's majority.

1930

November 3   Ran for reelection as Presiding Judge of Jackson County. Won by a majority of 58,000 votes. Continued his policies of reform and programs of improvements.

1932

March 29   Tom Pendergast, by this date, had taken over complete control of the Democratic party in the state of Missouri.

1933

October 1   Truman accepted a dollar-a-year appointment from Federal Emergency Relief Administrator Harry Hopkins as Re-Employment Director of Missouri.

1934

May 17   Filed for the Democratic Senatorial primary. Had received the endorsement of "Boss" Pendergast.

August 7   In a very tough and dirty primary election, Truman defeated two other candidates (John J. Cochran and Jacob L. Milligan) by a plurality of 44,000 votes.

November 5   Defeated an anti-New Deal Republican (incumbent Republican Senator Roscoe C. Patterson) in an extremely easy election by a plurality of 262,000 votes.

1935

January 3   Sworn into his Senate seat by Vice-President John Nance Garner. Truman was attired in a rented morning coat and striped pants.

January 25   Became member of Senate's Interstate Commerce Committee headed by Senator Burton K. Wheeler of Montana. Truman, eventually, became vice-chairman of this committee. Also appointed to the Appropriations Committee, and to the joint House-Senate Printing Committee. Trained by Wheeler in the art of investigation.

May 15   Introduced first public bill entitled, "A bill to provide for insurance by the Farm Credit Administration of mortgages on farm property, and for other purposes." It was referred by Vice-President Garner to the Committee on Banking and Currency, where it died.

July 5   Voted for the Wagner-Connery Labor Relations Bill. In fact, Truman voted for almost all of the various pieces of New Deal legislation between 1935 and 1938, with only a few exceptions.

August 28   As a member of the Interstate Commerce Committee, he helped to sponsor the Wheeler-Rayburn Public Utility Holding Company Act, which he also voted for, despite considerable pressure from business interests.

1937

July 22   Voted in support of President Roosevelt's Supreme Court reform proposal which was defeated by the Senate by a vote of 70 to 20.

1938

February 16   Cast his vote in support of the new Agricultural Adjustment Act.

June 23   Truman and Senator Warren Austin of Vermont were chiefly responsible for the passage of the Civil Aeronautics Act. They conducted the hearings on the Bill in the Civil Aeronautics Subcommittee, and wrote the Bill setting up an administrative director for the Civil Aeronautics Board.

1939

December 2　Introduced the Wheeler-Truman Bill proposing changes in the interstate commerce laws regulating the financing of the railroads. Truman had begun working on the problem in February, 1935.

1940

October 16　The Wheeler-Truman Bill was signed by President Roosevelt under the title of the Transportation Act of 1940.

February 4　Despite his accomplishments and his support of the New Deal, Truman was urged not to run for reelection. Pendergast had been sent to prison, and Truman was criticized for his ties with the discredited organization. Nevertheless, he filed for the Democratic primary.

June 15　Opened his campaign for reelection on the courthouse stairs in Sedalia, Missouri.

July 15　Truman served on the Missouri delegation to the Democratic National Convention in Chicago.

August 6　In a difficult, up-hill primary election, Truman defeated Maurice Milligan and Governor Lloyd Stark. His margin of victory was only 8,000 votes.

November 5　Reelected Senator over his Republican opponent Manville Davis. Truman had been vindicated, and was now a Senator on his own merit.

1941

January 3　Sworn into Senatorial office for a second time. When he walked onto the Senate floor that day, his colleagues gave him a standing ovation.

January 6　Washington D.C. stirring with activity. President Roosevelt who had been reelected, had concluded the "Destroyer Deal" with England, Congress had repealed the arms embargo, and the President had recommended Lend-Lease for the Allies. (Annual Message)

February 10　After having made a tour of 30,000 miles, checking hundreds of Army camps and defense plants, Truman rose in the

Senate chamber and denounced the defense program, calling it corrupt, inefficient and uneconomical. Submitted a resolution asking for an investigation of the defense program by the Senate which concurred.

February 17   Truman appointed chairman of Senate Special Committee to Investigate the National Defense Program (known as the Truman Committee). Other members included Senators Tom Connally, Carl Hatch, James Mead, Mon Wallgren, Joseph Ball and Owen Brewster.

April 15   First hearing of the Committee took place. The idea of the Committee was to conduct the investigation of the defense effort simultaneously with the war program in order that mistakes could be remedied before irretrievable damage was done. Truman remained as head of the Committee until 1944.

April 23   Committee made trip to Fort Meade, Maryland, to inspect that camp. This was only the first of several camps the Committee inspected in order to learn whether or not the War Department had made any emergency plans during the past twenty years.

April 25   As these investigations were getting under way, the United Mine Workers went on strike, threatening the entire defense program. Truman announced that if coal was not being taken from the ground within 24 hours, the Committee would summon all the representatives of the operators, and John L. Lewis in order to get them together to maintain coal production.

April 28   When both sides ignored Truman's threat, he ordered Lewis and 12 northern operators to appear before his committee. That night the deadlock was ended and a settlement made.

December 7   Japanese aircraft attacked United States military and naval bases at Pearl Harbor in the Hawaiian Islands precipitating American entry into World War II.

December 8   With only one dissenting vote, the United States Congress declared war on Japan.

December 10   Truman went to see General George C. Marshall to get his permission to join the regular army. Marshall told him he had a big enough job to do at the Capitol.

December 11   Germany and Italy declared war on the United States, which then recognized a state of war with these nations .

1942

January 15   Truman delivered to the Senate the first annual report of the Special Committee Investigating the National Defense Program. It showed waste, corruption, and inefficiency. During 1942 the Truman Committee uncovered even more staggering evidence of graft and waste.

1943

March 8   Truman appeared on the cover of *Time* magazine. The profile story was not entirely accurate, but it emphasized his importance to the war effort.

June 1   By this date, the Truman Committee had issued twenty-one reports covering an increasing variety of subjects.

1944

July 14   James Byrnes called from Washington to ask Truman to nominate him at the Democratic convention in Chicago. Byrnes claimed Roosevelt had decided on him as the new nominee for Vice-President.

July 19   Named chairman of the Missouri delegation at the convention.

July 20   Robert Hannegan told by Roosevelt that Truman is his selection for the Vice-Presidential nomination. Truman agreed to allow his name to be placed in nomination. Roosevelt nominated for a fourth term.

July 21   In a close convention election, Truman defeated Henry Wallace on the second ballot for the Democratic Vice-Presidential nomination. Truman's acceptance speech was only 92 words. Hannegan had been instrumental in getting the nomination for Truman.

August 3   Submitted resignation as chairman and member of the Senate Investigating Committee due to campaign commitments and politics.

August 31   Senator Tom Connally of Texas, at Lamar, Missouri, went through the ceremony of officially notifying Truman that he was the Democratic nominee for Vice-President.

September 4   Truman delivered pre-campaign Labor Day speech in Detroit. Had to give afternoon speech to the C.I.O., and evening speech to the A.F. of L. as the two unions were not on speaking terms.

September 6   Went to White House for conversation with Roosevelt concerning struggle with Republicans.

October 12   Began campaign tour in New Orleans. The tour carried Truman through Texas, New Mexico, up the Pacific Coast to Seattle, then eastward across the country to Massachusetts, down to New York and Washington, and finally back home to Missouri.

November 7   Roosevelt and Truman defeated the Republican candidates, Thomas E. Dewey and John W. Bricker, by a plurality of 3,596,227. The vote in the electoral college was 432 to 99.

November 8   Sent telegram to President Roosevelt congratulating him on the victory.

November 10   Flew to Washington, D.C. where he and Roosevelt triumphantly rode through the streets of the Capital to the White House.

1945

January 20   Henry Wallace, the retiring Vice-President, administered the oath of office to Truman. The inauguration took place on the south portico of the White House.

January 22   Took over as presiding officer of the Senate. Roosevelt had already left for the Yalta Conference.

January 26   Tom Pendergast died in Kansas City. Truman flew to Missouri for the funeral.

March 8   Saw President Roosevelt, but discussed nothing important. During Truman's 82 day period as Vice-President, Roosevelt was in Washington less than 30 days.

April 12   Roosevelt died in Warm Springs, Georgia. Truman took oath of office from Chief Justice Harlan F. Stone at 7:09 P.M. Gave first order as President, announcing that the United Nations Charter Conference would proceed on schedule in San Francisco. Asked Cabinet to remain for a short meeting and assured them he would carry out the policies of Roosevelt. After meeting, was informed privately about the atomic bomb by Secretary of War Henry L. Stimson.

FIRST TERM

April 13   Received briefing from Secretary of State Edward Stettinius on foreign affairs. Issued a proclamation of Roosevelt's death. Met with advisors all day.

April 14   Moved to Blair House diagonally across from the White House. Mrs. Roosevelt's accumulations of thirteen years still in the White House, and Truman insisted she take her time in moving out.

April 16   Addressed joint session of Congress. This was his first major speech as President.

April 22-23   At Blair House, discussed Soviet-American relations with Soviet Foreign Minister Vyacheslav Molotov. Scolded the Russian for violating the Yalta Agreement to establish a freely elected government in Poland. Also present was Andrei Gromyko, the Soviet Ambassador to the United States.

April 25   San Francisco United Nations Charter Conference opened. Truman addressed the delegates representing 50 nations.

May 1   Hitler committed suicide.

May 2   Berlin fell, and the German forces in Italy surrendered.

May 4   The German forces in the Netherlands, Denmark and north-west Germany surrendered.

May 7   Field Marshal Jodl signed the instrument of unconditional surrender of Germany in the Allied headquarters at Reims. The Trumans moved into the White House that evening.

May 8   V-E Day marked formal end of the war in Europe. In a radio address Truman informed the nation.

May 23   Appointed Tom C. Clark, Attorney-General, to replace Francis Biddle; Lewis Schwellenbach, Secretary of Labor, to replace Frances Perkins; and Clinton P. Anderson, Secretary of Agriculture to replace Claude R. Wickard.

May 24   Sent message to Congress requesting legislation for reorganization of the Executive branch.

May 27   Sent Harry Hopkins to Russia for talks with Stalin on termination of lend-lease, violation of Yalta Agreement concerning Poland, and possibility of a direct meeting of the Big Three in the near future. Stalin agreed to a conference to start in July.

June 5   German occupation zones were established by the European Advisory Commission meeting in London. West Germany was divided among the United States, Great Britain and France. Russia occupied East Germany while Berlin was divided among these four powers.

June 12   Truman ordered the withdrawal of United States troops into the American zone in Germany.

June 26   Addressed final session of the United Nations Charter Conference.

June 29   Announced that agreement had been reached between the Soviets and the United Nations concerning U.S. troop entry into Berlin, which was within the Russian zone.

June 30   Appointed Robert Hannegan, Post-Master General, to replace Frank C. Walker; and James F. Byrnes, Secretary of State, to replace Edward Stettinius.

July 3   Went in person to the Senate to submit the United Nations Charter for ratification. The Senate gave its approval on July 28 by a vote of 89 to 2.

July 7   Left from Newport News, Virginia on the U.S.S. *Augusta* for the Potsdam Conference.

July 16   Announced appointment of Fred Vinson as Secretary of the Treasury to replace Robert Morgenthau, Jr.

July 17-
August 2   Attended Potsdam Conference along with Joseph Stalin, Winston Churchill, and after July 28, Clement Attlee. Such matters as ending the war with Japan, world peace, post-war Germany, and the de-nazification of Germany were discussed. Polish German borders would be determined by final peace treaties; a Council of Foreign Ministers of the Big Five would prepare peace treaties; and Russia would not take reparations.

July 24   Truman made decision to use atomic bomb on a Japanese city if Japan did not surrender by July 30.

July 26   Ultimatum issued to Japan to surrender. It was refused.

July 28   The United Nations Treaty was accepted by the Senate.

August 6   First atomic bomb dropped on the Japanese city of Hiroshima. Truman received the news on board the *Augusta*.

August 7   Landed in the United States.

August 8   Russia declared war on Japan. Russian armies invaded Manchuria.

August 9   An atomic bomb was dropped on the Japanese city and naval base of Nagasaki.

August 14   Japanese accepted the Allied terms of surrender.

August 15   V-J Day proclaimed by Truman.

August 17   Ordered General Douglas MacArthur to temporarily divide Korea at the 38th parallel. The Soviets occupied the North while United States forces moved into the South.

August 21   Announced the end of Lend-Lease to the Allied nations.

August 29   Named General Douglas MacArthur Supreme Commander for the Allied powers in Japan. The occupation of Japan began, and did not end until 1951.

August 31   Wrote to Prime Minister Attlee requesting that the British government allow 100,000 more Jewish refugees to enter Palestine.

September 2   The Japanese Premier and military leaders signed the formal surrender on the board the U.S.S. *Missouri* in Tokyo Bay.

The Democratic Republic of Vietnam (North Vietnam) was created under communist leader, Ho Chi Minh.

September 6   Truman sent Congress a 21-point reconversion program requesting legislation for the post-war world.

September 11-
October 2   The first meeting of the Council of Foreign Ministers took place in London. It failed as the ministers could not agree on terms for peace treaties in Italy and the Balkan states.

September 18   Issued statement assuring American people that servicemen will be brought home as soon as possible.

September 21   Secretary of War Henry L. Stimson resigned.

September 22   Sent telegram to Premier Josef Stalin requesting him to abide by Postdam Agreement concerning French and Chinese participation in discussion of the Balkan situation.

September 24   Appointed Robert P. Patterson, Secretary of War.

September 28   Issued two proclamations and two executive orders asserting jurisdiction of the United States government over the natural resources of the continental shelf.

October 3   Sent message to Congress urging that a national plan for control of atomic energy be enacted into law.

October 4   Asked Congress for the establishment of a Domestic Atomic Energy Commission.

October 11   Ordered American Air Force transports to ferry Chiang Kai-Shek's troops into territory formerly held by the Japanese, as war between Nationalists and Communists began.

October 19   Invited General Douglas MacArthur to return to the United States to receive plaudits of a grateful nation.

October 22   Recommended to Congress a program of universal military training.

October 24   United Nations Charter went into effect.

October 27   Commissioned the aircraft carrier, U.S.S. *Franklin Delano Roosevelt* in New York City.

              Issued statement on the "Fundamentals of American Foreign Policy" in New York City's Central Park.

November 5   Called conference of leading labor and management officials to Washington to develop new approach to solving industrial crises.

November 15   Issued Joint Declaration on Atomic Energy with Prime Minister Attlee and Prime Minister MacKenzie King of Canada, providing for cooperation among the three powers.

November 19   Sent message to Congress recommending the establishment of a National Compulsary Health Insurance program financed through payroll and other deductions.

November 20   The Nuremberg Trials began. Twenty three Nazi officials were tried for crimes against humanity. Of these, 18 were convicted and 11 were sentenced to death. Supreme Court Justice Robert H. Jackson acted as prosecutor for the United States.

November 21 The United Auto Workers struck against General Motors. The first post-war strike and the first of a series during Truman's Administration. This one lasted 113 days.

November 23 Instructed Secretary of State James F. Byrnes to add the problem of Iran to Cabinet meeting agenda.

November 27 Requested that Ambassador Patrick J. Hurley return to China immediately.

November 30 Truman announced that he favored civilian and not military control over atomic energy in the United States.

December 3 Appeared before Congress and asked for legislation to create fact-finding boards to investigate labor disputes. Congress refused, but Truman set up the boards by an Executive Order.

December 6 The United States loaned $3.7 billion to Great Britain.

December 10 Appointed American members to the Anglo-American committee which conducted an investigation of the Palestine problem.

December 15 Sent General George C. Marshall to China as Special Ambassador to help establish a united, democratic China.

December 16-
December 26 Second meeting of the Council of Foreign Ministers took place in Moscow.

December 19 Recommended to Congress the reorganization of the armed forces into a single department.

December 20 Signed Executive Department Reorganization Bill.

Was quite pleased when the Senate defeated amendments to the United Nations Participation Act which would have required Congressional approval for the use of American troops in United Nations actions.

December 22   Issued directive concerning new measures to be taken to facilitate the entry of displaced persons under the quota system.

December 31   Abolished National War Labor Board and created, in its place, the Wage Stabilization Board.

1946

January 3   Addressed nation on the radio, concerning the dangers of dropping price controls.

January 10   United Nations General Assembly met for the first time in London. Trygve Lie of Norway was selected as the first Secretary General.

January 14   Delivered State of the Union Address.

January 19   Iran charged in the Security Council of the United Nations that the Soviets had kept troops in Iran in violation of the agreed-upon withdrawal date.

January 20   Issued executive order establishing the Control Intelligence Group which was renamed the Central Intelligence Agency in 1947.

Appointed Rear Admiral Sidney W. Souers the first Director of the C.I.A.

January 21   A three month strike by the United Steel Workers began.

February 12   Ordered General Marshall to expedite removal of American military forces from China.

February 13   Secretary of the Interior, Harold Ickes resigned, and Truman appointed Julius Krug as the new Secretary.

February 14   Issued executive order permitting temporary adjustments in price control increases.

February 20   Signed Employment Act designed to achieve full employment.

February 21   Created Office of Economic Stabilization, and named Chester Bowles its first Director.

February 28   Truman and Secretary of State James F. Byrnes announced a "get tough policy" regarding the Russians.

March 1   Appointed Famine Emergency Committee. Named ex-President Herbert Hoover as Chairman.

March 5   Winston Churchill delivered a Green Foundation Lecture at Westminster College in Fulton, Missouri at the invitation of Truman who promised to take him out and introduce him. In this speech, Churchill introduced the phrase, "Iron Curtain."

March 6   Sent note to Stalin expressing his disapproval of Soviet actions in Iran.

France recognized the Democratic Republic of Vietnam as part of the Indochinese Federation and the French Union. The others members were Laos and Cambodia.

March 15   Met with Marshall in Washington to discuss situation in China.

March 24   Threatened to send American naval forces to Mediterranean if Soviets did not remove troops from Iran as agreed to at Potsdam Conference.

March 24-30   Stalin removed Soviet troops.

April 1   United Mine Workers went out on strike.

April 20   The Anglo-American Committee of Inquiry recommended the termination of the British mandate in Palestine and its transfer to a United Nations trusteeship. It also called for the admittance into Palestine of 100,000 European Jews, and the creation of a state protecting both Jews and Arabs. Both Jews and Arabs rejected the plan.

April 21   Truman refused to endorse the Anglo-American Committee's plan for Palestine, preferring to wait for United Nation's action in the matter.

April 25   The Truman Administration's plan to unite Germany (involving inspection) was turned down by the Soviet Union.

May 8   The joint American-Soviet commission in Korea was ended.

May 16   Sent message to Attlee concerning Palestine problem.

May 17   Sent telegrams to heads of Arab states assuring them that the United States would not take any independent action concerning the settlement of the Palestine question.

May 21   Truman ordered government takeover of mines. They were returned to the mine owners in June, 1947.

May 22   Signed Emergency Housing Bill to provide for construction of 2,700,000 units for veterans within 2 years.

Met with disgruntled Railway Workers Union representatives in an attempt to avoid a strike.

May 24   Announced he would ask Congress to authorize the army to run the railroads.

May 25   Strike settled, but labor angry at Truman for his actions.

Requested joint session of Congress to pass strong emergency legislation to cope with strikes affecting the government or national interest.

May 27   Truman announced the suspension of military dismantling in the American Zone of Germany.

June 1   Appointed John W. Snyder, Secretary of the Treasury.

June 7-30   Nationalist and Communist Chinese signed a truce in Manchuria.

June 11   Vetoed Case Bill dealing with punitive measures against labor unions involved in strikes.

June 14   The Soviets rejected the Baruch Plan proposed by the United States delegate to the United Nations Atomic Energy Commission, Bernard Baruch. The plan would have established an International Atomic Development Authority with power to own all hazardous atomic energy activities, and the right of unlimited inspection.

June 19 Refused Soviet demands for destruction of all American atomic bombs as a condition for atomic energy talks.

June 26 Signed Philippines Military Assistance Act.

June 28 Accepted resignation of Chester Bowles as Director of Office of Economic Stabilization.

July 1 Atomic bomb dropped at Island of Bikini.

July 5 Atomic bomb dropped at Eniwetok.

July 12 Appointed Dr. John Davidson Clark, Leon H. Keyserling, and Edwin G. Houise to first Council of Economic Advisers.

July 15 Signed British Loan Bill extending original foreign aid package of 1945.

July 25 Signed bill extending price control for one more year.

July 27 Sent letter to Stalin recommending a common policy with respect to the world coal crisis.

August 1 Approved the McMahon Act sponsored by Senator Brien McMahon of Connecticut, setting up a five man Atomic Energy Commission.

August 2 Signed Legislative Reorganization Act reducing the number of Congressional committees and providing funds for the legislative budget.

August 10 Sent message to Chiang Kai-Shek stating that American efforts for a political settlement in China have failed.

August 12 Announced he would not support the Anglo-American Committee's plan for Palestine.

August 31 Submitted to Congress a detailed preliminary program for national military security.

September   A massive maritime strike ensued which closed all ports in
5-20   the United States.

September 6   The Truman Administration accused the Soviets of not
                 living up to the Potsdam agreements.

September 20 Dismissed Henry A. Wallace as Secretary of Agriculture.
                 Appointed W. Averell Harriman to this post.

October 14   Announced ending of price controls on meat.

October 15   Most price controls ended.

October 25   Issued proclamation declaring a state of emergency because
                 of the housing shortage.

                 Authorized the free importation of lumber.

October 28   Appointed David E. Lilienthal, Director of the Atomic
                 Energy Commission.

November 5   Republicans gained control of both houses of Congress.
                 This was the Eightieth Congress.

November 6   Ordered the ending of all wartime wage and price controls
                 except those on rent.

November 20 A second coal strike was called for by John L. Lewis despite
                 a Federal injunction barring such an action.

November 23 Fighting began between France and North Vietnam.

November 25 Issued Executive Order creating the President's Temporary
                 Commission on Employee Loyalty.

December 2   Announced that the United States and Great Britain had
                 merged their zones in Germany.

December 5   Appointed Committee to investigate and report on status
                 of civil rights in America. Named Charles E. Wilson,
                 chairman of committee.

December 7   Coal strike settled. Lewis fined by a federal court.

December 20   Met with Advisory Commission on Universal Military Training.

December 27   Announced that settlements had been made with seven nations (excluding the Soviet Union) on lend-lease repayments.

1947

January 1   Atomic Energy Commission began operations.

January 6   Delivered State of the Union Address.

General Marshall returned from China as United States peace efforts there failed.

January 12   Replaced James Byrnes with George Marshall as Secretary of State.

January 15   Announced plans to have a balcony built leading off his second floor White House study.

January 29   Truman announced he was abandoning mediation in China between the Nationalists and the Communists.

January 30   Announced the introduction of new economic policies in Japan to strengthen that nation.

January 31   Asked Congress to extend the Second War Powers Act.

February 14   Truman's mother (94 years old) fractured her hip.

February 19   Recommended to Congress the repeal of a number of temporary statutes still in effect by virtue of the emergencies proclaimed by Roosevelt in 1939 and 1941.

February 21   Great Britain announced that she could no longer provide economic and military assistance to Greece.

February 24   Met with General John R. Hodge for talks concerned with economic distress and political unrest in Korea.

February 26   Transmitted to Congress his draft of the National Security Act of 1947 to bring Army, Navy and Air Force under one department.

February 27   Announced that he had decided to extend economic aid to Greece and Turkey.

March 9   Visited Mexican President Miguel Aleman in Mexico City.

March 10   Met with group of Congressional leaders to discuss the Greek-Turkish aid program.

March 10-
April 24   Foreign Minister's Conference held in Moscow once more. No agreement was reached on the German question as the Soviets insisted on a centralized government for a united Germany and the United States desired a federal system.

March 12   Issued Truman Doctrine calling for the containment of Soviet expansion. Asked Congress for $400 million dollars for aid to Greece and Turkey.

March 16   Margaret Truman made her singing debut with the Detroit Symphony Orchestra. Was given a very bad review prompting Truman to castigate the critics.

March 22   Truman issued Loyalty Order for investigation of employees in the Executive branch of the Federal service.

                   Issued Civil Rights Message to Congress.

March 25   Replaced Robert P. Patterson with Kenneth C. Royall as Secretary of War.

March 31   Signed "First Decontrol Act of 1947" removing a number of wartime statutes.

April 23   The Truman Doctrine was endorsed by the Senate.

May 8   Under-Secretary of State, Dean Acheson, publicly advocated essentials of the European Recovery Program.

May 9   The Truman Doctrine was endorsed by the House of Representatives.

May 15   United Nations General Assembly established a committee to deal with the Palestine problem.

May 19   Recommended to Congress the establishment of a comprehensive health program for the nation.

May 22   Signed Greek-Turkish Aid Bill in Kansas City, Missouri.

June 5   The Marshall Plan was launched by Secretary of State George C. Marshall while delivering the commencement address at Harvard University.

June 20   Vetoed Taft-Hartley Act, sponsored by Representative Fred Hartley and Senator Robert A. Taft, who were both Republicans. The act provided that both labor and management had to give sixty days notice for the termination of a contract; the government could delay a strike for eighty days if public health or safety were endangered; the "closed shop" was prohibited; secondary boycotts, jurisdictional strikes, excessive dues and featherbedding were prohibited; and required union leaders to take a non-Communist oath.

June 23   Congress passed the Taft-Hartly Act over Truman's veto.

June 29   Attended NAACP convention, and detailed his civil rights program for the delegates.

July 3   Foreign Minister Molotov walked out of a meeting in Paris on the Marshall Plan charging that it was an "imperialist plot."

July 7   Signed Act of Congress establishing the Hoover Commission on the organization of the Executive branch.

July 11-
August 24   Sent General Albert C. Wedemeyer to the Far East to appraise the situation in China and Korea.

July 11   Wedemeyer urged United States military aid to the Nationalists in a report made public in 1949.

July 12   Marshall Plan Conference held in Paris. Sixteen nations set up the Committee for European Economic Cooperation.

July 15   Signed "Second Decontrol Act of 1947," which removed the remaining wartime emergency legislation.

July 18   Signed Presidential Succession Act.

July 25   Signed National Security Act which established a unified Department of Defense and created the National Security Council.

July 26   Truman's mother died.

July 27   Appointed James V. Forrestal, the first Secretary of Defense.

July 29-
  October 15   Paris Peace Conference held, at which treaties with Axis satellites were agreed upon. The treaties were finally signed in New York on February 10, 1948.

August 22   On a "Good Neighbor" trip to Brazil, Truman signed a Mutual Defense Assistance Pact in Rio de Janeiro.

Loyalty check began.

September 2   A Treaty of Reciprocal Assistance was drawn up at the Inter-American Conference in Rio de Janeiro, Brazil. The United States Senate ratified the treaty on December 8, 1947.

October 5   Asked Congress for power to control commodity exchanges.

October 9   Instructed State Department to support the United Nation's Palestinian Partition Plan.

October 29   The Wilson Committee on Civil Rights reported its findings to Truman in a paper entitled, "To Secure these Rights."

November 17   Called Congress into special session to deal with the economic crisis in Western Europe, and inflation prevention at home.

November 19   Met with Jewish leader Chaim Weizmann to discuss partition of Palestine.

November 26   Appointed Jesse Donaldson, Postmaster General.

November 29 General Assembly of the United Nations passed Palestinian Partition Plan.

December 19 Submitted to Congress his $17,000,000,000 European Recovery Program.

December 28 Henry Wallace announced formation of a third party called the Progressive Party.

1948

January 7 Delivered State of the Union Address.

February 2 Sent to Congress a ten-point program on civil rights concerned with ending segregation in public schools and accomodations, and reducing discrimination in employment.

February 17 Approved State Department proposal concerning eventuality of war in the Middle East.

February 19 Presented civil rights proposals to assembled Democrats at Jefferson-Jackson Day Dinner at Little Rock, Arkansas.

March 6 Agreement reached in London by the United States, Great Britain, France, Belgium, Luxembourg, and the Netherlands on the formation of a federal government in West Germany, and the participation of that government in the European Recovery Program.

March 17 Addressed joint session of Congress on the Cold War, and asked for a strengthening of the National Defense, restoration of Selective Service, and further legislative action on E.R.P.

March 19 First government injunction under the Taft-Hartley Act was issued against a strike at the Oak Ridge Atomic Energy Plant.

March 27 Promulgated new statement of functions for the Department of Defense and its separate branches.

March 30-
May 2   The Charter of the Organization of American States was drawn up at Bogota, Columbia. It was to become effective December 13, 1951.

April 3   Signed European Recovery Act, providing $17 billion to be used for the economic recovery of Europe.

April 5   Named Paul G. Hoffman as Economic Cooperation Administrator with cabinet rank.

April 17   Truman delivered first non-prepared speech at the meeting of the American Society of Newspaper Editors.

April 20   John L. Lewis and the United Mine Workers were fined for contempt of court during another coal strike.

April 23   Appointed Charles Sawyer, Secretary of Commerce.

May 14-
November 30 War between the newly created state of Israel and the Arab League ensued. The fighting was ended by a United Nations cease-fire agreement.

May 15   Gave *de facto* recognition to the new state of Israel.

June 3   Began "non-political" speaking tour of California.

June 5   South Vietnam created as part of the French Union.

June 11   The Vandenberg Resolution proposed by Senator Arthur H. Vandenberg of Michigan was adopted. It stated that the United States could associate itself in peacetime with countries outside the Western Hemisphere in collective security arrangements.

June 18   Truman returned to Washington after speaking in cities across the nation.

               Ordered currency reforms in the American Zone of Berlin.

June 24   Signed new Selective Service Act.

Soviets began total blockade of Berlin, and Truman ordered improvised "air-lift" to the beleagured city.

At the Republican National Convention in Philadelphia, Governor Thomas E. Dewey of New York was nominated for the Presidency and Governor Earl Warren of California for the Vice-Presidency.

June 25   Met with Cabinet to discuss Berlin Crisis.

Authorized issuance of new visas for the admission of 205,000 European displaced persons.

June 26   Ordered all planes in American European Command to service Berlin's needs until Soviets removed blockade.

July 2   Approved Vandenberg Resolution.

July 12   Democratic National Convention opened in Philadelphia.

July 13   Agreed on Senator Alben W. Barkley of Kentucky as running mate.

July 15   Truman and Barkley nominated by the Democrats. When the Convention adopted a strong civil rights plank, the delegates from Mississippi and Alabama walked out.

July 17   Southern Democrats met at Birmingham, Alabama, and formed the States' Rights Party (Dixiecrats). They nominated Governor J. Strom Thurmond of South Carolina for President and Governor Fielding L. Wright of Mississippi for Vice-President on a platform calling for racial segregation.

July 22   Met with General Lucius D. Clay at the White House to discuss Berlin situation.

The Progressive Party meeting in Philadelphia nominated Henry A. Wallace for President and Senator Glenn H. Taylor of Idaho for Vice-President and urged a conciliatory policy toward Russia.

July 26   Called Congress into special session ("Turnip Day" special session) to enact his domestic programs, to pass his inflation-control bill, and to repeal the Taft-Hartley Act. It accomplished very little.

Issued executive order barring segregation in the armed forces and prohibited discrimination in federal employment.

July 27   Sent six-page message to Congress demanding constructive social legislation.

July 31   The Gallup, Crossley and Roper polls indicated an overwhelming Dewey victory in November.

August 3   Whittaker Chambers, admitted former Communist courier, named Alger Hiss as a member of a pre-war Communist apparatus in Washington.

August 5   Challenged Eightieth Congress to take action on his anti-inflation bill.

August 8   Appointed Maurice Tobin, Secretary of Labor.

August 15   Recognized the Republic of Korea, and ordered an end to American military government in the South.

August 16   Signed Anti-Inflation Control Act.

August 23   Instructed Ambassador Walter Bedell Smith to meet with Stalin on the Berlin situation.

September 6   Began campaign on Labor Day in Detroit, Michigan.

September 17   Truman began a cross country speaking tour that would take him 21,928 miles, and to almost 200 cities. Truman announced that he was going to give the Republicans "hell" in his speeches.

September 19   Dewey started campaign tour across the country in his *Victory Special*. Overconfidant, he waged an indifferent and ineffective campaign.

September 23-26   Truman campaigned in Texas with newly nominated Senator, Lyndon B. Johnson. He visited Houston, Dallas, San

Antonio, Waco and other cities, paying his respects to ex-Vice-President John Nance Garner at Uvalde where a crowd of 5,000 persons greeted him at 5 A.M.

September 28 Reaffirmed the "Israel Plank" of the Democratic Platform in Oklahoma City, Oklahoma.

October 1 Denounced Eightieth Congress in Denver, Colorado, calling the Republicans "a bunch of old mossbacks . . . living back in 1890".

October 5 Summoned Tom Connolly and Arthur H. Vandenberg to White House to discuss proposed Vinson Mission to Russia which was to be an attempt at reconciliation with the Soviets.

October 15 Truman drew 50,000 people at an Indianapolis, Indiana, rally on a cold night.

October 16 At the Chicago Stadium, 30,000 persons jammed inside to hear Truman speak. He told the crowd that he had the Republicans on the run, and that he was going to win the election.

October 28 Attended giant rally in Madison Square Garden, New York City.

October 30 Delivered his last campaign speech at a mammoth rally in St. Louis, Missouri.

October 31 Returned to Independence, Missouri, to await outcome of the election.

November 2 Truman defeated Dewey by a popular vote of 24,105,812 to 21,970,065, and an Electoral vote of 303 to 189. States Rights candidate J. Strom Thurmond of South Carolina received 39 Electoral votes, while Progressive Party candidate Henry Wallace received no electoral votes.

Negro, labor and farmer votes helped Truman retain the Presidency. As he boarded the train in St. Louis on his way back to Washington, Truman happily held aloft a copy of the Chicago *Tribune* with the headline: DEWEY DEFEATS TRUMAN.

November 7   Went to Key West, Florida, for well-earned vacation.

November 29   Offered Israel financial assistance.

December 15   Alger Hiss was indicted on two counts of perjury by a Federal Grand Jury in New York.

SECOND TERM
1949

January 1   Marshall resigned as Secretary of State and was replaced by Dean Acheson.

January 5   Delivered State of the Union Address dealing with his Fair Deal program for improved housing, education, civil rights, and health.

January 19   Congress raised the President's salary to $100,000.

January 20   Truman inaugurated. His inauguration address introduced the Point-Four plan which was a bold program for making the benefits of American scientific and industrial progress available for the improvement and growth of underdeveloped areas.

January 31   Extended *de jure* recognition to the state of Israel.

March 5   Proposed to Congress revisions in the National Security Act.

Judith Coplon, Justice Department employee, and Valentin Gubichev, Soviet consular official were arrested for espionage. Both were found guilty on March 7, 1950.

March 18   Replaced Secretary of Defense, James Forrestal, with Louis A. Johnson.

April 4   Attended signing of North Atlantic Pact in Washington, D.C., and addressed the representatives of the eleven signatory nations. The Pact established the North Atlantic Treaty Organization (NATO) for collective defense against aggression.

April 8   Ordered the United States zone in Germany to be merged with those of Great Britain and France.

April 12   Sent North Atlantic Treaty to Senate for ratification. The Senate ratified treaty by a vote of 82 to 13 on July 21, 1949.

May 1   Began "non-political" tour across the country to gain backing for the Fair Deal.

May 12   Berlin blockade ended, and Truman terminated the air-lift.

May 18   Truman appointed John J. McCloy High Commissioner of West Germany.

June 20   Signed Reorganization Act of 1949. Based on the work of the Herbert Hoover Commission, the act allowed the President to reorganize the executive branch with Congressional approval.

June 24   Sent special message to Congress concerning the implementation of the Point-Four program. Recommended an initial appropriation of $45,000,000.

July 8   Alger Hiss' first trial ended in a hung jury.

July 15   Signed the Housing Act, the goal of which was a decent house for every American family.

July 21   The Senate ratified the North Atlantic Treaty. The vote was 82 to 13.

July 25   Signed North Atlantic Treaty ratification.

August 5   With Truman's approval, the State Department issued a white paper that blamed the Communist victory in China on Chiang Kai-shek's inefficient, corrupt government. It also stated that the United States had done everything possible to save China from the Reds.

August 10   Signed National Security Act Amendments into law.

                Named General Omar Bradley, Chairman, Joint Chiefs of Staff.

August 24   The North Atlantic Treaty Organization began operations.

September 21 Truman ordered the termination of United States military government in Germany.

September 22 Signed Mutual Defense Assistance Bill which provided for military aid to NATO allies in case of aggression.

September 23 Announced to the nation that the Soviets had perfected an atomic bomb.

October 1   A Communist regime under Chairman Mao Tse-tung was established in China. Although Great Britain and Russia extended immediate recognition of the new government in China, Truman refused to take such action.

October 14   A Federal court in New York convicted the eleven top leaders of the American Communist Party for violation of the Smith Act.

November 17 Alger Hiss was found guilty of perjury at his second trial, and was sentenced to five years in prison.

December 8   Chinese Communists were victorious in their struggle with the Nationalists. Chiang Kai-shek and the Naionalists fled to Taiwan (Formosa).

1950

January 4   Delivered State of the Union Address.

January 12   Secretary of State Dean Acheson stated that Korea and Formosa were not included within the United States defense perimeter.

January 24   Signed bill raising minimum wage to 75 cents an hour.

January 26   Approved defense agreement with Korea.

January 27   Formally approved NATO defense arrangements.

January 31   Ordered construction of a Hydrogen bomb in the United States.

February 7   Truman recognized Laos, Cambodia and South Vietnam as independent states.

February 9   Senator Joseph R. McCarthy of Wisconsin in a speech at Wheeling, West Virginia charged that there were 209 Communists in the State Department. Truman refuted this accusation.

April 28   The National Science Foundation Act was passed by Congress to establish a foundation to promote scientific research and teaching.

May 8   The United States began sending economic and military aid to the South Vietnamese government.

June 5   Signed International Development Act (Point-Four).

June 24   Dedicated Friendship Airport outside of Baltimore.

June 25   North Korea invaded South Korea by crossing the 38th parallel. United Nations Security Council, with Russia absent, declared North Korea the aggressor.

June 27   Truman ordered United States air and naval forces into Korea, as well as the Seventh Fleet to the Formosa Straits to prevent Chinese Communists from invading Taiwan.

June 28   Appointed General Douglas MacArthur head of American forces in Korea. MacArthur flew from Tokyo to Korea.

June 29   Met with National Security Council to decide on Korean policy.

June 30   Ordered United States ground forces into Korea.

Draft extended to July, 1951.

July 7   Asked Congress to enlarge the draft.

July 8   Truman named MacArthur Supreme Commander of United Nations forces in Korea.

July 19   Asked Congress to remove limitations on the size of the armed forces.

Announced that it would be necessary to raise taxes.

July 20 Proposed partial mobilization.

Professor Owen Lattimore of Johns Hopkins University was cleared by a Senate Sub-Committee of being a Communist. In March, 1950, Senator McCarthy had accused Lattimore of being a Communist agent.

July 31 Ordered four national guard divisions to be inducted into active Federal service.

August 3 Sent Averell Harriman to Tokyo for talks with MacArthur on Far Eastern political situation.

August 8 Sent special message to Congress concerning the internal security of the United States.

August 26 Seized the railroads to prevent an impending strike. They were not returned by the government until May 23, 1952.

August 26 Told advisors he intends to relieve MacArthur of command and replace him with Bradley.

August 28 Signed bill extending Social Security benefits.

September 1 Truman spoke to the nation over the radio on the Korean situation.

September 6 Signed General Appropriations Act of 1951.

September 8 Signed Defense Production Act.

Issued executive order establishing the International Development Advisory Board.

September 12 Removed Secretary of Defense Louis Johnson and replaced him with General Marshall.

September 15 D-Day at Inchon, South Korea.

September 22 Vetoed McCarran Internal Security Act sponsored by Senator Pat McCarran of Nevada. The act made it illegal to conspire to establish a totalitarian dictatorship in the

United States. In addition, members of Communist organizations could not hold Federal appointive offices or receive passports. Communist organizations had to register with the Attorney General's office, and former members of totalitarian organizations were barred from entering the United States.

September 23 Congress passed the Internal Security Act over Truman's veto.

September 28 Seoul, capital of South Korea, was liberated.

September 30 Truman cruised with some of his advisers on Korea, in the yacht *Williamsburg* on the Potomac River.

October 1 Allied forces crossed the 38th parallel into the North.

October 14 Truman met with MacArthur at Wake Island for talks.

October 17 Announced to reporters in San Francisco that his Wake Island meeting with MacArthur was unsatisfactory.

Octbober 19 Pyongyang, capital of North Korea, captured by United Nations forces.

October 26 Chinese Communist troops intervene in Korean fighting.

November 1 Two Puerto Rican Nationalists, Oscar Collazo and Griselio Torresola, attempted to assassinate Truman at Blair House, Washington, D.C.

November 6 Truman went to Kansas City, Missouri, to await results of Congressional elections the next day.

November 7 Democrats retained control of both Houses of Congress, but Republicans gained a number of seats.

Not wishing to risk the chance of war with the Soviet Union, the Joint Chiefs of Staff denied General MacArthur's request to bomb Communist bases in Manchuria.

November 14 Appointed Dr. Henry Garland Bennett as administrator of the Technical Cooperation Administration.

December 4-7 Met with Prime Minister Attlee for talks on Korea. Truman said that he would not back down before the Russians on Korea.

December 5 Ordered that no speeches, press releases, or public statements by government or military officials, concerning foreign policy, should be made until they were cleared by the Department of State.

December 11 Met with National Security Council to discuss a cease-fire resolution passed in the United Nations.

December 16 Named General Dwight D. Eisenhower Supreme Commander of NATO forces (SHAPE).

Proclaimed State of National Emergency.

December 20 Truman's foreign policy attacked by Herbert Hoover.

December 20 Appointed Charles E. Wilson, President of General Motors, Director of the Office of Economic Stabilization.

December 23 Signed a Mutual Defense Agreement with France, South Vietnam, Laos, and Cambodia.

December 29 MacArthur advised that U.N. forces attack Red China.

December 30 Truman refused to allow MacArthur to use Nationalist Chinese troops in Korea.

1951

January 1 United Nations forces driven out of Seoul.

Congress granted Truman power to freeze prices in an attempt to stem inflation.

January 5 Established United Defense Fund to provide a pool of financial resources for the military defense of the free world.

January 8 Delivered State of the Union Address.

January 23 Appointed Commission on Internal Security and Individual Rights, and named Admiral Chester W. Nimitz as Chairman.

February 2   Recommended to Congress a "Pay as We Go Tax Program."

February 5   Fulbright Committee issued its report stating that an influence ring with White House contacts existed.

Eventually charges of corruption were levelled against Harry H. Vaughn, a military aide, and General T. Lamar Caudle, the Assistant Attorney General. Truman fired both men, but a number of other scandals rocked the Truman Administration.

February 26   Signed Twenty-Second Amendment to the Constitution which provided that the President, henceforth, would be limited to two terms or a maximum of ten years. It would not have applied to Truman.

March 7   MacArthur issued a statement to the press ridiculing Truman's policies concerning Korea.

March 24   Truman ordered MacArthur not to make any further independent statements concerning foreign policy, after MacArthur ordered the Chinese to surrender.

MacArthur issued a statement threatening to invade Communist China.

April 5   MacArthur expressed view that it was "sheer folly" not to use Chinese Nationalist troops in Korea. This was revealed in a letter to Representative Joseph W. Martin.

Julius and Ethel Rosenberg were sentenced to death after their conviction for espionage of atomic secrets. They died in the electric chair on July 19, 1953.

April 11   Truman relieved MacArthur of his command in Korea and replaced him with General Matthew B. Ridgeway.

June 16   Signed an extension of the Trade Agreements Act of 1934 for a two year period.

June 19   On Truman's request, Congress extended the draft.

June 23   Held talks with Jacob Malik, the Soviet representative to the United Nations, on possibility of a cease-fire in Korean War.

June 27   Truman's removal of MacArthur was vindicated by the Senate as it urged a continuation of a limited war in Korea.

July 7   Negotiations for a cease-fire in the Korean fighting began in Kaesong. After many difficulties an armistice was finally concluded on July 27, 1953.

August 1   Cancelled tariff concessions to all nations under Soviet domination.

September 1   Signed tripartite agreement with Australia and New Zealand providing for mutual assistance in the event of aggression.

September 8   Signed Japanese Peace treaty.

September 13   Appointed Robert Lovett, Secretary of Defense.

October 10   Signed Mutual Security Act which combined funds for the Marshall Plan, Point-Four, and the Mutual Defense Act.

October 19   The state of war with Germany was officially ended by Congress.

October 22   Signed amendments to the Taft-Hartley Act.

November 1   The United Steelworkers of America announced that when their contract expired in 1952, they would seek wage increases.

November 19   Informed his staff that he would not be a candidate in 1952.

December 22   Referred the dispute between the United Steelworkers and the steel companies to the Wage Stabilization Board.

December 29   Issued executive order establishing the President's Committee on the Health Needs of the Nation.

1952

January 3   Truman, in an address to the nation, explained the purpose and function of the Commission on the Health Needs of the nation.

January 5-8   Met with Winston Churchill in Washington, D.C. for talks concerned with the world situation.

January 9   Delivered State of the Union Address.

January 22   Met with Governor Adlai E. Stevenson of Illinois at White House to offer him the Presidential nomination. Stevenson refused.

February 1   Appointed Newbold Morris of New York to investigate corruption among Federal officials.

February 28   Senate Sub-Committee to Investigate Crime, headed by Senator Estes Kefauver of Tennessee, reported. Wide public attention was attracted by its televised hearings.

March 3   Signed congressional resolution approving new Constitution for Puerto Rico as well as Commonwealth status.

March 4   Truman again asked Stevenson if he would accept the Democratic nomination. Again Stevenson refused.

March 20   Steel companies refused to abide by a Wage Mediation Board award.

March 29   At a Jefferson-Jackson Day Dinner in Washington, D.C., Truman publicly announced that he would not be a candidate in the 1952 Presidential election.

April 3   Removed Attorney General J. Howard McGrath, supposedly for lack of cooperation in a campaign to clean up the corruption in the government.

April 4   Appointed J.P. McGranery new Attorney General.

April 6   Announced that the United States was manufacturing a hydrogen bomb.

April 7   Truman issued an executive order to seize the steel mills because of an impending strike in the steel industry.

April 8   Reported to Congress concerning his actions in the steel strike.

April 28	At his press conference, Truman insisted that the government had the right to seize the steel mills because of the State of National Emergency.
April 29	Federal Judge David Pine ruled that Truman's seizure of the steel mills was unconstitutional.
May 7	Summoned Benjamin Fairless of United States Steel and Philip Murray, President of the C.I.O., to the White House to work out a settlement in the steel strike.
May 16	Ordered the termination of the German High Commission.
May 29	Vetoed Tidelands Oil Bill which would have given oil rights off California, Texas and Louisiana to those states.
June 2	The United States Supreme Court in the *Youngstown Sheet and Tube Company vs. Sawyer* case upheld Judge Pine's decision invalidating Truman's seizure of the steel mills.
	Issued executive order to Secretary of Commerce, Charles Sawyer, to return mills to the steel companies.
June 3-24	The Steel Workers of America went out on strike. Some 560,000 men were involved.
June 4	Truman was furious. He castigated the Union leaders and requested permission from Congress to seize the steel mills. The request was denied.
June 10	Asked Congress for legislation to permit the President to seize strike bound plants. Congress refused.
June 14	Ordered construction of atomic submarine, U.S.S. *Nautilus.*
June 25	Vetoed McCarran-Walter Immigration Act sponsored by Senator Pat McCarran and Representative Francis Walter of Pennsylvania. The Act retained the 1924 national-origins system and intensified the screening and deporting of aliens.
June 30	Signed one year extention of the Defense Production Act.

June 27   Congress passed the McCarran-Walter Immigration Act over Truman's veto.

July 7-11   The Republican National Convention meeting at Chicago, nominated Dwight D. Eisenhower and Richard M. Nixon. The platform accused the Democrats of appeasement of Communism.

July 21-26   Democratic National Convention met in Chicago.

July 24   Signed act enlarging self-government for Puerto Rico.

Commuted death sentence of Oscar Collazo who had killed a White House guard during the assassination attempt of 1950.

Truman intervened to settle another impending strike by the United Steelworkers of America.

Stevenson now asked Truman if he would agree to Stevenson's name being placed in nomination. Truman agreed.

Steel strike ended.

July 25   Truman flew to Chicago to address the Democratic National Convention.

Stevenson and Senator John J. Sparkman of Alabama were nominated.

August 2   Signed West German Peace Contract.

August 4   ANZUS (Pacific) Council was created by the mutual security pact between the United States, Australia and New Zealand at Honolulu.

October 4   Campaigned at Oakland, California, in behalf of Adlai Stevenson.

November 1   First hydrogen bomb was dropped in the Pacific. Truman announced this event to the nation.

November 4   Eisenhower and Nixon defeated Stevenson and Sparkman, 442 electoral votes to 89. The popular vote was 33.9 million for Eisenhower, 27.3 million for Stevenson.

November 5   Invited President-elect Eisenhower to Washington for talks.

November 18   Met with Eisenhower at White House for talks concerning the transition of the government.

December 5   Flew to Independence, Missouri, for the funeral of his mother-in-law.

December 18   Truman's Commission on the Health Needs of the Nation recommended a program falling between the compulsory health insurance proposals of the Truman Administration and a limited, voluntary, prepaid plan advocated by the American Medical Association.

1953

January 7   Delivered State of the Union Address.

January 15   Truman made his Farewell Address to the American people on radio and television.

January 16   Issued executive order setting aside the submerged lands of the Continental Shelf as a naval petroleum reserve.

January 20   President Eisenhower inaugurated.

Truman left Washington in the afternoon, by train, for his home in Missouri.

RETIREMENT

1953

February 1   Opened an office in the Federal Reserve Bank building in Kansas City, Missouri.

March 12-29   Truman vacationed at Coconut Island in Hawaii.

October 21   Refused an audience with President Eisenhower, when "Ike" visited Kansas City, Missouri.

1954

June 15   Truman underwent a gall bladder operation in a Kansas City hospital.

1955

August 5   Volume I of his *Memoirs* was published.

1956

January 22 Volume II of his *Memoirs* was published.

April 21   Attended wedding of his daughter, Margaret, to Clifton Daniel, a writer for the *New York Times.*

May 7-26   Truman vacationed in Europe, and visited with Winston Churchill at Chartwell.

August 13-17 Attended Democratic National Convention in Chicago, where he backed the candidacy of W. Averell Harriman.

1957

February 6   Injured himself in a fall on an icy walk in Independence, Missouri.

February 11-
March 1   Vacationed in Miami, Florida.

June 5   Grandson, Clifton Truman Daniel, was born.

July 7   The Harry S Truman Library in Independence was dedicated.

August 25   Advocated a tougher Soviet policy in a speech in Kansas City.

September 17 The Truman Library was opened to the public.

December 27 Called Eisenhower-Dulles Report on NATO Conference, "State Department gobbeldygook."

1958

February 3   Filmed a TV interview for C.B.S.

February 7   The interview was shown on nationwide TV.

February 19   Truman accepted position of Chubb fellow at Yale.

April 27   Visited St. Lawrence Seaway Project.

September 17 Accepted United States government pension.

December 9   Stated he would like to be appointed United States Senator from Missouri to fill out Stuart Symington's term if Symington were elected President or Vice-President in 1960.

1959

February 5   Rejected suggestion to run for Congress in 1960.

April 13   Lectured on the Presidency at Columbia University.

May 9   Truman's 75th birthday was marked by parties held in 66 cities. Sixteen cities were linked together by closed circuit television to hear his remarks from Independence.

May 20   Second grandson, William Wallace Daniel, born.

October 21   Attended the funeral of George C. Marshall in Washington, D.C.

1960

January 21   The Truman Chair in American Civilization established at Brandeis University.

April 25   Truman's new book *Truman Speaks* was published.

May 3   Named delegate from Missouri to the Democratic National Convention to be held in Los Angeles, California.

May 14   Announced in Chicago that he was supporting Stuart Symington for the Presidential nomination.

June 10   Truman's second book of the year, *Mr. Citizen,* was published.

June 27   Announced he would not attend the Democratic National Convention because it was "rigged" and resigned as a delegate.

July 16   When John F. Kennedy was nominated, Truman sent a telegram to the Convention urging Democrats to unite behind Kennedy and Johnson.

July 30   Agreed to campaign for Kennedy.

October 11   Began nationwide campaign tour in Texarkana, Texas.

1961

January 20   Attended Kennedy inauguration.

February 10-
March 4   Vacationed in Bermuda.

May 28   Truman attended White House signing of Latin American Aid Bill.

June 26   Signed with Talent Associates—Paramount Ltd. to appear in 26 one hour documentary programs.

November 11 Took Eisenhower on a tour of the Truman Library.

November 19 Attended funeral of Sam Rayburn in Texas.

1962

August 11   Attended dedication of the Hoover Library in West Branch, Iowa.

September 18 Awarded Philadelphia Freedom Medal.

November 11 Attended funeral of Mrs. Eleanor Roosevelt in New York.

1963

January 19   Underwent hernia operation in Kansas City.

March 4   Third grandson born.

November 26 Attended funeral of President John F. Kennedy in Washington.

1964

March 13   Attended funeral of King Paul I of Greece as President Johnson's official representative.

May 9   Addressed the Senate, and became first ex-President to address that body while it was in formal session.

June 26   Awarded highest South Korean decoration on the 14th anniversary of the Korean War.

October 14   Fractured two ribs in a fall at his home in Independence, and was rushed to the hospital.

October 23   Left hospital to rest at home. Condition reported satisfactory.

1965

January 20   Sent congratulatory wire to President Lyndon Johnson on inauguration day.

July 31   Attended President Johnson's signing of the Medicare Bill at the Truman Library.

1966

January 20   Hebrew University in Jerusalem announced it was going to construct the Harry S Truman Center for the Advancement of Peace. Truman stated that he planned to attend the ground-breaking ceremonies.

January 21   President Johnson presented Medicare Card #1 to Truman at Independence.

July 31-
August 6   Truman entered a hospital in Kansas City for treatment of a colitis condition.

1967

November 11   Truman held Veteran's Day reunion with twenty-five World War I friends at his home in Independence.

1968

February 28-
April 2   Vacationed at the home of J. J. Spottswood in Key West, Florida.

May 4   President Johnson briefed Truman, in Independence, on proposed Vietnam peace talks.

November 6   Voted on Election Day in Independence.

ADDRESS BEFORE A JOINT SESSION OF CONGRESS
April 16, 1945

In a somber mood, Truman paid tribute to the dead President Roosevelt, and told Congress of his determination to continue the war to a victorious conclusion.

Mr. Speaker, Mr. President, Members of the Congress:

It is with a heavy heart that I stand before you, my friends and colleagues, in the Congress of the United States.

Only yesterday, we laid to rest the mortal remains of our beloved President, Franklin Delano Roosevelt. At a time like this, words are inadequate. The most eloquent tribute would be a reverent silence.

Yet, in this decisive hour, when world events are moving so rapidly, our silence might be misunderstood and might give comfort to our enemies.

In His infinite wisdom, Almighty God has seen fit to take from us a great man who loved, and was beloved by, all humanity.

No man could possibly fill the tremendous void left by the passing of that noble soul. No words can ease the aching hearts of untold millions of every race, creed and color. The world knows it has lost a heroic champion of justice and freedom.

Tragic fate has thrust upon us grave responsibilities. We *must* carry on. Our departed leader never looked backward. He looked forward and moved forward. That is what he would want us to do. That is what America *will* do....

Our forefathers came to our rugged shores in search of religious tolerance, political freedom and economic opportunity. For those fundamental rights, they risked their lives. We well know today that such rights can be preserved only by constant vigilance, the eternal price of liberty!

Within an hour after I took the oath of office, I announced that the San Francisco Conference would proceed.[1] We will face the problems of peace with the same courage that we have faced and mastered the problems of war.

In the memory of those who have made the supreme sacrifice—in the memory of our fallen President—*we shall not fail!*

It is not enough to yearn for peace. We must work, and if necessary, fight for it. The task of creating a sound international organization is complicated and difficult. Yet, without such organization, the rights of man on earth cannot be protected. Machinery for the just settlement of international differences must be found. Without such machinery the entire world will have to remain an armed camp. The world will be doomed to deadly conflict devoid of hope for real peace.

Fortunately, people have retained hope for a durable peace. Thoughtful people have always had faith that ultimately justice *must* triumph. Past experience surely indicates that, without justice, an enduring peace becomes impossible.

In bitter despair, some people have come to believe that wars are inevitable. With tragic fatalism, they insist that wars have always been, of necessity, and of necessity wars always will be. To such defeatism, men and women of good will must not and can not yield. The outlook for humanity is not so hopeless.

During the dark hours of this horrible war, entire nations were kept going by something intangible—hope! When warned that abject submission offered the only salvation against overwhelming power, hope showed the way to victory.

Hope has become the secret weapon of the forces of liberation!

Aggressors could not dominate the human mind. As long as hope remains, the spirit of man will *never* be crushed.

But hope alone was not and is not sufficient to avert war. We must not only have hope but we must have faith enough to work with other peace-loving nations to maintain the peace. Hope was not enough to beat back the aggressors as long as the peace-loving nations were unwilling to come to each other's defense. The aggressors were beaten back only when the peace-loving nations united to defend themselves.

If wars in the future are to be prevented the nations must be united in their determination to keep the peace under law.

Nothing is more essential to the future peace of the world than continued cooperation of the nations which had to muster the force necessary to defeat the conspiracy of the Axis powers to dominate the world.

While these great states have a special responsibility to enforce the peace, their responsibility is based upon the obligations resting upon all states, large and small, not to use force in international relations except in the defense of law. The responsibility of the great states is to serve and not to dominate the world.

To build a foundation of enduring peace we must not only work in harmony with our friends abroad, but we must have the united support of our own people.

Even the most experienced pilot cannot bring a ship safely into harbor, unless he has the full cooperation of the crew. For the benefit of all, every individual must do his duty.

I appeal to every American, regardless of party, race, creed, or color, to support our efforts to build a strong and lasting United Nations Organization.

You, the Members of the Congress, surely know how I feel. Only with your help can I hope to complete one of the greatest tasks ever assigned to a public servant. With Divine guidance, and your help, we will find the new passage to a far better world, a kindly and friendly world, with just and lasting peace.

With confidence, I am depending upon all of you.

To destroy greedy tyrants with dreams of world domination, we cannot continue in successive generations to sacrifice our finest youth.

In the name of human decency and civilization, a more rational method of deciding national differences *must* and *will* be found!

America must assist suffering humanity back along the path of peaceful progress. This will require time and tolerance. We shall need also an abiding faith in the people, the kind of faith and courage which Franklin Delano Roosevelt always had!

Today, America has become one of the most powerful forces for good on earth. We must keep it so. We have achieved a world leadership which does not depend solely upon our military and naval might.

We have learned to fight with other nations in common defense of our freedom. We must now learn to live with other nations for our mutual good. We must learn to trade more with other nations so that there may be—for our mutual advantage—increased production, increased employment and better standards of living throughout the world.

May we Americans all live up to our glorious heritage.

In that way, America may well lead the world to peace and prosperity.

At this moment, I have in my heart a prayer. As I have assumed my heavy duties, I humbly pray Almighty God, in the words of King Solomon:

"Give therefore thy servant an understanding heart to judge thy people, that I may discern between good and bad; for who is able to judge this thy so great a people?"

I ask only to be a good and faithful servant of my Lord and my people.

SPECIAL MESSAGE TO CONGRESS ON THE ORGANIZATION
OF THE EXECUTIVE BRANCH
May 24, 1945

With the end of the European phase of the war, and the imminent collapse of the Japanese empire, Truman sought to retain some of the more favorable features of executive control that had been developed during the war-time period. He believed that the executive branch of government could benefit greatly from this type of organization during peace-time.

To the Congress of the United States:

The Congress has repeatedly manifested interest in an orderly transition from war to peace. It has legislated extensively on the subject, with foresight and wisdom.

I wish to draw the attention of the Congress to one aspect of that transition for which adequate provision has not as yet been made. I refer to the conversion of the Executive Branch of the Government.

Immediately after the declaration of war the Congress, in Title I of the First War Powers Act, 1941, empowered the President to make necessary adjustments in the organization of the Executive Branch with respect to those matters which relate to the conduct of the present war. This authority has been extremely valuable in furthering the prosecution of the war. It is difficult to conceive how the executive agencies could have kept continuously attuned to the needs of the war without legislation of this type.

The First War Powers Act expires by its own terms six months after the termination of the present war. Pending that time, Title I will be of very substantial further value in enabling the President to make such additional temporary improvements in the organization of the Government as are currently required for the more effective conduct of the war.

However, further legislative action is required in the near future, because the First War Powers Act is temporary, and because, as matters now stand, every step taken under Title I will automatically revert upon the termination of the Title, to the pre-existing status.

Such automatic reversion is not workable. I think that the Congress has recognized that fact, particularly in certain provisions of section 10 of the War Mobilization and Reconversion Act of 1944. In some instances it will be necessary to delay reversion beyond the period now provided by law, or to stay it permanently. In other instances it will be necessary to modify actions heretofore taken under Title I and to continue the resulting arrangement beyond the date of expiration of the Title. Automatic reversion will result in the re-establishment of some agencies that should not be re-established. Some adjustments of permanent character need to be made, as exemplified by the current proposal before the Congress with respect to the subsidiary corporations of the Reconstruction Finance Corporation. Some improvements heretofore made in the Government under the First War Powers Act, as exemplified by the reorganization of the Army under Executive Order No. 9082, should not be allowed to revert automatically or at an inopportune time.

I believe it is realized by everyone—in view of the very large number of matters involved and the expedition required in their disposition, that the problems I have mentioned will not be met satisfactorily unless the Congress provides for them along the general lines indicated in the message.

Quite aside from the disposition of the war organization of the Government, other adjustments need to be made currently and continuously in the Government establishment. From my experience in the Congress, and from a review of the pertinent developments for a period of forty years preceding that experience, I know it to be a positive fact that, by and large, the Congress cannot deal effectively with numerous organizational problems on an individual item basis. The Congressional Record is replete with expressions of members of the Congress, themselves, to this effect. Yet it is imperative that these matters be dealt with continuously if the Government structure is to be reasonably wieldy and manageable, and be responsive to proper direction by the Congress and the President on behalf of the people of this country. The question is one that goes directly to the adequacy and effectiveness of our Government as an instrument of democracy.

Suitable reshaping of those parts of the Executive Branch of the Government which require it from time to time is necessary and desirable from every point of view. A well organized Executive Branch will be more efficient than a poorly organized one. It will help materially in making manageable the Government of this great nation. A number of my predecessors have urged the Congess to take steps to make the Executive Branch more business-like and efficient. I welcome and urge the cooperation of Congress to the end that these objectives may be attained.

Experience has demonstrated that if substantial progress is to be made in these regards, it must be done through action initiated or taken by the President. The results achieved under the Economy Act (1932), as amended, the Reorganization Act of 1939, and Title I of the First War Powers Act, 1941, testify to the value of Presidential initiative in this field.

Congressional ciriticisms are heard, not infrequently, concerning deficiencies in the Executive Branch of the Government. I should be less than frank if I failed to point out that the Congress cannot consistently advance such criticisms and at the same time deny the President the means of removing the causes as the root of such criticisms.

Accordingly, I ask the Congress to enact legislation which will make it possible to do what we all know needs to be done continuously and expeditiously with respect to improving the organization of the Executive Branch of the Government. In order that the purposes which I have in mind may be understood, the following features are suggested: (a) the legislation should be generally similar to the Reorganization Act of 1939, and part 2 of Title I of that Act should be utilized intact, (b) the legislation should be of permanent duration, (c) no agency of the Executive Branch should be exempted from the scope of the legislation, and (d) the legislation should be sufficiently broad and flexible to permit of any form of organizational adjustment, large or small, for which necessity may arise.

It is scarcely necessary to point out that under the foregoing arrangement (a) necessary action is facilitated because initiative is placed in the hands of the President, and (b) necessary control is reserved to the Congress since it may, by simple majority vote of the two Houses nullify any action of the President which does not meet with its approval. I think, further, that the Congress recognizes that particular arrangement as its own creation, evolved within the Congress out of vigorous efforts and debate extending over a period of two years and culminating in the enactment of the Reorganization Act of 1939.

Therefore, bearing in mind what the future demands of all of us, I earnestly ask the Congress to enact legislation along the foregoing lines without delay.

HARRY S TRUMAN

ON THE USE OF THE A-BOMB AT HIROSHIMA
August 6, 1945

An Atomic bomb with an explosive force of 20,000 tons of TNT was dropped on the Japanese city of Hiroshima on August 6, 1945. Truman recognized the potentialities of such power for both good and evil purposes, and thus informed the American people.

SIXTEEN HOURS AGO an American airplane dropped one bomb on Hiroshima, an important Japanese Army base. That bomb had more power than 20,000 tons of T.N.T. It had more than two thousand times the blast power of the British "Grand Slam" which is the largest bomb ever yet used in the history of warfare.

The Japanese began the war from the air at Pearl Harbor. They have been repaid many fold. And the end is not yet. With this bomb we have now added a new and revolutionary increase in destruction to supplement the growing power of our armed forces. In their present form these bombs are now in production and even more powerful forms are in development.

It is an atomic bomb. It is a harnessing of the basic power of the universe. The force from which the sun draws its power has been loosed against those who brought war to the Far East.

Before 1939, it was the accepted belief of scientists that it was theoretically possible to release atomic energy. But no one knew any practical method of doing it. By 1942, however, we knew that the Germans were working feverishly to find a way to add atomic energy to the other engines of war with which they hoped to enslave the world. But they failed. We may be grateful to Providence that the Germans got the V-I's and V-2's late and in limited quantities and even more grateful that they did not get the atomic bomb at all. The battle of the laboratories held fateful risks for us as well as the battles of the air, land and sea, and we have now won the battle of the laboratories as we have won the other battles.

Beginning in 1940, before Pearl Harbor, scientific knowledge useful in war was pooled between the United States and Great Britain, and many priceless helps to our victories have come from that arrangement. Under that general policy the research on the atomic bomb was begun. With American and British scientists working together we entered the race of discovery against the Germans.

The United States had available the large number of scientists of distinction in the many needed areas of knowledge. It had the tremendous industrial and financial resources necessary for the project and they could be devoted to it without undue impairment of other vital war work. In the United States the laboratory work and the production plants, on which a substantial start had already been made, would be out of reach of enemy bombing, while at that time Britain was exposed to constant air attack and was still threatened with the possibility of invasion. For these reasons Prime Minister Churchill and President Roosevelt agreed that it was wise to carry on the project here. We now have two great plants and many lesser works devoted to the production of atomic power. Employment during peak construction numbered 125,000 and over 65,000 individuals are even now engaged in operating the plants. Many have worked there for two and a half years. Few know what they have been producing. They see great quantities of material going in and they see nothing coming out of these plants, for the physical size of the explosive charge is exceedingly small. We have spent two billion dollars on the greatest scientific gamble in history—and won.

But the greatest marvel is not the size of the enterprise, its secrecy, nor its cost, but the achievement of scientific brains in putting together infinitely complex pieces of knowledge held by many men in different fields of science into a workable plan. And hardly less marvelous has been the capacity of industry to design, and of labor to operate, the machines and methods to do things never done before so that the brain child of many minds came forth in physical shape and performed as it was supposed to do. Both science and industry worked under the direction of the United States Army, which achieved a unique success in managing so diverse a problem in the advancement of knowledge in an amazingly short time. It is doubtful if such another combination could be got together in the world. What has been done is the greatest achievement of organized science in history. It was done under high pressure and without failure.

We are now prepared to obliterate more rapidly and completely every productive enterprise the Japanese have above ground in any city. We shall destroy their docks, their factories, and their communications. Let there be no mistake; we shall completely destroy Japan's power to make war.

It was to spare the Japanese people from utter destruction that the ultimatum of July 26 was issued at Potsdam. Their leaders promptly rejected the ultimatum. If they do not now accept our terms they may expect a rain of ruin from the air, the like of which has never been seen on this earth. Behind this air attack will follow sea and land forces in such numbers and power as they have not yet seen and with the fighting skill of which they are already well aware.

The Secretary of War, who has kept in personal touch with all phases of the project, will immediately make public a statement giving further details.

His statement will give facts concerning the sites at Oak Ridge near Knoxville, Tennessee, and at Richland near Pasco, Washington, and an installation near Santa Fe, New Mexico. Although the workers at the sites have been making materials to be used in producing the greatest destructive force in history they have not themselves been in danger beyond that of many other occupations, for the utmost care has been taken of their safety.

The fact that we can release atomic energy ushers in a new era in man's understanding of nature's forces. Atomic energy may in the future supplement the power that now comes from coal, oil, and falling water, but at present it cannot be produced on a basis to compete with them commercially. Before that comes there must be a long period of intensive research.

It has never been the habit of the scientists of this country or the policy of this Government to withhold from the world scientific knowledge. Normally, therefore, everything about the work with atomic energy would be made public.

But under present circumstances it is not intended to divulge the technical processes of production or all the military applications, pending further examination of possible methods of protecting us and the rest of the world from the danger of sudden destruction.

I shall recommend that the Congress of the United States consider promptly the establishement of an appropriate commission to control the production and use of atomic power within the United States. I shall give further consideration and make further recommendations to the Congress as to how atomic power can become a powerful and forceful influence towards the maintenance of world peace.

ON ATOMIC ENERGY
October 3, 1945

*Two months after the first Atomic bomb was used by the United
States, Truman outlined a series of proposals to Congress concerned with the future development of Atomic energy.*

To the Congress of the United States:

Almost two months have passed since the atomic bomb was used against
Japan. That bomb did not win the war, but it certainly shortened the war.
We know that it saved the lives of untold thousands of American and Allied
soldiers who would otherwise have been killed in battle.

The discovery of the means of releasing atomic energy began a new era in
the history of civilization. The scientific and industrial knowledge on which
this discovery rests does not relate merely to another weapon. It may some
day prove to be more revolutionary in the development of human society
than the invention of the wheel, the use of metals, or the steam or internal
combustion engine.

Never in history has society been confronted with a power so full of potential danger and at the same time so full of promise for the future of man
and for the peace of the world. I think I can express the faith of the American
people when I say that we can use the knowledge we have won, not for the
devastation of war, but for the future welfare of humanity.

To accomplish that objective we must proceed along two fronts—the
domestic and the international.

The first and most urgent step is the determination of our domestic policy
for the control, use and development of atomic energy within the United
States.

We cannot postpone decisions in this field. The enormous investment
which we made to produce the bomb has given us the two vast industrial
plants in Washington and Tennessee, and the many associated works
throughout the country. It has brought together a vast organization of
scientists, executives, industrial engineers and skilled workers—a national
asset of inestimable value.

The powers which the Congress wisely gave to the Government to wage
war were adequate to permit the creation and development of this enterprise as a war project. Now that our enemies have surrendered, we should
take immediate action to provide for the future use of this huge investment
in brains and plant. I am informed that many of the people on whom depend
the continued successful operation of the plants and the further development
of atomic knowledge, are getting ready to return to their normal pursuits. In
many cases these people are considering leaving the project largely because
of uncertainty concerning future national policy in this field. Prompt action

to establish national policy will go a long way towards keeping a strong organization intact.

It is equally necessary to direct future research and to establish control of the basic raw materials essential to the development of this power whether it is to be used for purposes of peace or war. Atomic force in ignorant or evil hands could inflict untold disaster upon the nation and the world. Society cannot hope even to protect itself—much less to realize the benefits of the discovery—unless prompt action is taken to guard against the hazards of misuse.

I therefore urge, as a first measure in a program of utilizing our knowledge for the benefit of socieity, that the Congress enact legislation to fix a policy with respect to our existing plants, and to control all sources of atomic energy and all activities connected with its development and use in the United States.

The legislation should give jurisdiction for these purposes to an Atomic Energy Commission with members appointed by the President with the advice and consent of the Senate.

The Congress should lay down the basic principles for all the activities of the Commission, the objectives of which should be the promotion of the national welfare, securing the national defense, safeguarding world peace and the acquisition of further knowledge concerning atomic energy.

The people of the United States know that the overwhelming power we have developed in this war is due in large measure to American science and American industry, consisting of management and labor. We believe that our science and industry owe their strength to the spirit of free inquiry and the spirit of free enterprise that characterize our country. The Commission, therefore, in carrying out its functions should interfere as little as possible with private research and private enterprise, and should use as much as possible existing institutions and agencies. The observance of this policy is our best guarantee of maintaining the pre-eminence in science and industry upon which our national well-being depends.

All land and mineral deposits owned by the United States which constitute sources of atomic energy, and all stock piles of materials from which such energy may be derived, and all plants or other property of the United States connected with its development and use should be transferred to the supervision and control of the Commission.

The Commission should be authorized to acquire at a fair price, by purchase or by condemnation, any minerals or other materials from which the sources of atomic energy can be derived, and also any land containing such minerals or materials, which are not already owned by the United States.

The power to purchase should include real and personal property outside the limits of the United States.

The Commission should also be authorized to conduct all necessary research, experimentation, and operations for the further development and use of atomic energy for military, industrial, scientific, or medical purposes. In these activities it should, of course, use existing private and public institutions and agencies to the fullest practicable extent.

Under appropriate safeguards, the Commission should also be permitted to license any property available to the Commission for research, development and exploitation in the field of atomic energy. Among other things such licensing should be conditioned of course upon a policy of widespread distribution of peacetime products on equitable terms which will prevent monopoly.

In order to establish effective control and security, it should be declared unlawful to produce or use the substances comprising the sources of atomic energy or to import or export them except under conditions prescribed by the Commission.

Finally, the Commission should be authorized to establish security regulations governing the handling of all information, material and equipment under its jurisdiction. Suitable penalties should be prescribed for violating the security regulations of the Commission or any of the other terms of the Act.

The measures which I have suggested may seem drastic and far-reaching. But the discovery with which we are dealing involves forces of nature too dangerous to fit into any of our usual concepts.

The other phase of the problem is the question of the international control and development of this newly discovered energy.

In international relations as in domestic affairs, the release of atomic energy constitutes a new force too revolutionary to consider in the framework of old ideas. We can no longer rely on the slow progress of time to develop a program of control among nations. Civilization demands that we shall reach at the earliest possible date a satisfactory arrangement for the control of this discovery in order that it may become a powerful and forceful influence towards the maintenance of world peace instead of an instrument of destruction . . .

HARRY S TRUMAN

ON THE FUNDAMENTALS OF AMERICAN FOREIGN POLICY
October 27, 1945

This was the first important statement of foreign policy after Truman's return from the Potsdam Conference. Point ten anticipated the subsequent fourth point of the Fair Deal program of 1949.

. . . 1. We seek no territorial expansion or selfish advantage. We have no plans for aggression against any other state, large or small. We have no objective which need clash with the peaceful aims of any other nation.

2. We believe in the eventual return of sovereign rights and self-government to all peoples who have been deprived of them by force.

3. We shall approve no territorial changes in any friendly part of the world unless they accord with the freely expressed wishes of the peoples concerned.

4. We believe that all peoples who are prepared for self-government should be permitted to choose their own form of government by their own freely expressed choice, without interference from any foreign source. That is true in Europe, in Asia, in Africa, as well as in the Western Hemisphere.

5. By the combined and cooperative action of our war Allies, we shall help the defeated enemy states establish peaceful, democratic governments of their own free choice. And we shall try to attain a world in which Nazism, Fascism, and military aggression cannot exist.

6. We shall refuse to recognize any government imposed upon any nation by the force of any foreign power. In some cases it may be impossible to prevent forceful imposition of such a government. But the United States will not recognize any such government.

7. We believe that all nations should have the freedom of the seas and equal rights to the navigation of boundary rivers and waterways and of rivers and waterways which pass through more than one country.

8. We believe that all states which are accepted in the society of nations should have access on equal terms to the trade and the raw materials of the world.

9. We believe that the sovereign states of the Western Hemisphere, without interference from outside the Western Hemisphere, must work together as good neighbors in the solution of their common problems.

10. We believe that full economic collaboration between all nations, great and small, is essential to the improvement of living conditions all over the world, and to the establishment of freedom from fear and freedom from want.

11. We shall continue to strive to promote freedom of expression and freedome of religion throughout the peace-loving areas of the world.

12. We are convinced that the preservation of peace between nations requires a United Nations Organization composed of all the peace-loving nations of the world who are willing jointly to use force if necessary to insure peace.

That is the foreign policy which guides the United States now. That is the foreign policy with which it confidently faces the future.

It may not be put into effect tomorrow or the next day. But none the less, it is our policy; and we shall seek to achieve it. It may take a long time, but it is worth waiting for, and it is worth striving to attain. . . .

ON THE ESTABLISHMENT OF A DEPARTMENT OF DEFENSE
December 19, 1945

While a Department of Defense coordinating the army, navy, and air force into a single National Military Establishment was not created until 1947, Truman urged the creation of such an agency as early as 1945.

To the Congress of the United States:

In my message of September 6, 1945, I stated that I would communicate with the Congress from time to time during the current session with respect to a comprehensive and continuous program of national security. I pointed out the necessity of making timely preparation for the Nation's long-range security now—while we are still mindful of what it has cost us in this war to have been unprepared.

On October 23, 1945, as part of that program, there was presented for your consideration a proposal for universal military training. It was based upon the necessities of maintaining a well-trained citizenry which could be quickly mobilized in time of need in support of a small professional military establishement. Long and extensive hearings have now been held by the Congress on this recommendation. I think that the proposal, in principle, has met with the overwhelming approval of the people of the United States.

We are discharging our armed forces now at the rate of 1,500 a month. We can with fairness no longer look to the veterans of this war for any future military service. It is essential therefore that universal training be instituted at the earliest possible moment to provide a reserve upon which we can draw if, unhappily, it should become necessary. A grave responsibility will rest upon the Congress if it continues to delay this most important and urgent measure.

Today, again in the interest of national security and world peace, I make this further recommendation to you. I recommend that the Congress adopt legislation combining the War and Navy Departments into one single Department of National Defense. Such unification is another essential step— along with universal training— in the development of a comprehensive and continuous program for our future safety and for the peace and security of the world.

One of the lessons which have most clearly come from the costly and dangerous experience of this war is that there must be unified direction of land, sea and air forces at home as well as in all other parts of the world where our Armed Forces are serving.

We did not have that kind of direction when we were attacked four years ago—and we certainly paid a high price for not having it.

In 1941, we had two completely independent organizations with no well-established habits of collaboration and cooperation between them.

If disputes arose, if there was failure to agree on a question of planning or a question of action, only the President of the United States could make a decision effective on both. Besides, in 1941, the air power of the United States was not organized on a par with the ground and sea forces.

Our expedient for meeting these defects was the creation of the Joint Chiefs of Staff. On this Committee sat the President's Chief of Staff and the chiefs of the land forces, the naval forces, and the air forces. Under the Joint Chiefs were organized a number of committees bringing together personnel of the three services for joint strategic planning and for coordination of operations. This kind of coordination was better than no coordination at all, but it was in no sense a unified command.

In the theaters of operation, meanwhile, we went further in the direction of unity by establishing unified commands. We came to the conclusion— soon confirmed by experience—that any extended military effort required over-all coordinated control in order to get the most out of the three armed forces. Had we not early in the war adopted this principle of a unified command for operations, our efforts, no matter how heroic, might have failed.

But we never had comparable unified direction or command in Washington. And even in the field, our unity of operations was greatly impaired by the differences in training, in doctrine, in communication systems, and in supply and distribution systems, that stemmed from the division of leadership in Washington.

It is true, we were able to win in spite of these handicaps. But it is now time to take stock, to discard obsolete organizational forms and to provide for the future the soundest, the most effective and the most economical kind of structure for our armed forces of which this most powerful Nation is capable.

I urge this as the best means of keeping the peace.

No nation now doubts the good will of the United States for the maintenance of a lasting peace in the world. Our purpose is shown by our efforts to establish an effective United Nations Organization. But all nations—and particularly those unfortunate nations which have felt the heel of the Nazis, the Fascists or the Japs—know that desire for peace is futile unless there is also enough strength ready and willing to enforce that desire in any emergency. Among the things that have encouraged aggression and the spread of war in the past have been the unwillingness of the United States realistically to face this fact, and her refusal to fortify her aims of peace before the forces of aggression could gather in strength.

Now that our enemies have surrendered it has again become all too apparent that a portion of the American people are anxious to forget all about the war, and particularly to forget all the unpleasant factors which are required to prevent future wars.

Whether we like it or not, we must all recognize that the victory which we have won has placed upon the American people the continuing burden of responsibility for world leadership. The future peace of the world will depend in large part upon whether or not the United States shows that it is really determined to continue in its role as a leader among nations. It will depend upon whether or not the United States is willing to maintain the physical strength necessary to act as a safeguard against any future aggressor. Together with the other United Nations, we must be willing to make the sacrifices necessary to protect the world from future aggressive warfare. In short, we must be prepared to maintain in constant and immediate readiness sufficient military strength to convince any future potential aggressor that this Nation, in its determination for a lasting peace, means business.

We would be taking a grave risk with the national security if we did not move now to overcome permanently the present imperfections in our defense organization. However great was the need for coordination and unified command in World War II, it is sure to be greater if there is any future aggression against world peace. Technological developments have made the Armed Services much more dependent upon each other than ever before. The boundaries that once separated the Army's battlefield from the Navy's battlefield have been virtually erased. If there is ever going to be another global conflict, it is sure to take place simultaneously on land and sea and in the air, with weapons of even greater speed and range. Our combat forces must work together in one team as they have never been required to work together in the past.

We must assume, further, that another war would strike much more suddenly than the last, and that it would strike directly at the United States. We cannot expect to be given the opportunity again to experiment in organization and in ways of teamwork while the fighting proceeds. True preparedness now means preparedness not alone in armaments and numbers of men, but preparedness in organization also. It means establishing in peacetime the kind of military organization which will be able to meet the test of sudden attack quickly and without having to improvise radical readjustment in structure and habits.

The basic question is what organization will provide the most effective employment of our military resources in time of war and the most effective means for maintaining peace. The manner in which we make this transition in the size, composition, and organization of the armed forces will determine the efficiency and cost of our national defense for many years to come.

Improvements have been made since 1941 by the President in the organization of the War and Navy Departments, under the War Powers Act. Unless the Congress acts before these powers lapse, these Departments will revert to their prewar organizational status. This would be a grievous mistake . . .

HARRY S TRUMAN

STATE OF THE UNION MESSAGE
January 21, 1946

In this very long address, Truman discussed primarily the various programs concerned with reconversion. He called for a more balanced economy, full employment, industrial peace, and international cooperation among other things.

To the Congress of the United States:

. . . Since our programs for this period which combines war liquidation with reconversion to a peacetime economy are inevitably large and numerous it is imperative that they be planned and executed with the utmost efficiency and the utmost economy. We have cut the war program to the maximum extent consistent with national security. We have held our peacetime programs to the level necessary to our national well-being and the attainment of our postwar objectives. Where increased programs have been recommended, the increases have been held as low as is consistent with these goals. I can assure the Congress of the necessity of these programs. I can further assure the Congress that the program as a whole is well within our capacity to finance it. All the programs I have recommended for action are included in the Budget figures.

For these reasons I have chosen to combine the customary Message on the State of the Union with the annual Budget Message. . . .

I am also transmitting herewith the Fifth Quarterly Report of the Director of War Mobilization and Reconversion. It is a comprehensive discussion of the present state of the reconversion program and of the immediate and long-range needs and recommendations.

This constitutes, then, as complete a report as I find it possible to prepare now. It constitutes a program of government in relation to the Nation's needs.

With the growing responsibility of modern government to foster economic expansion and to promote conditions that assure full and steady employment opportunities, it has become necessary to formulate and determine the Government program in the light of national economic conditions as a whole. In both the executive and the legislative branches we must make arrangements which will permit us to formulate the Government program in that light. Such an approach has become imperative if the American political and economic system is to succeed under the conditions of economic instability and uncertainty which we have to face. The Government needs to assure business, labor, and agriculture that Government policies will take due account of the requirements of a full employment economy. The lack of that assurance would, I believe, aggravate the economic instability. . .

I. FROM WAR TO PEACE—THE YEAR OF DECISION

. . . In his last Message on the State of the Union, delivered one year ago, President Roosevelt said:

"This new year of 1945 can be the greatest year of achievement in human history.

"1945 can see the final ending of the Nazi-Fascist reign of terror in Europe.

"1945 can see the closing in of the forces of retribution about the center of the malignant power of imperialist Japan.

"Most important of all—1945 can and must see the substantial beginning of the organization of world peace."

All those hopes, and more, were fulfilled in the year 1945. It was the greatest year of achievement in human history. It saw the end of the Nazi-Fascist terror in Europe, and also the end of the malignant power of Japan. And it saw the substantial beginning of world organization for peace. These momentous events became realities because of the steadfast purpose of the United Nations and of the forces that fought for freedom under their flags. The plain fact is that civilization was saved in 1945 by the United Nations.

Our own part in this accomplishment was not the product of any single service. Those who fought on land, those who fought on the sea, and those who fought in the air deserve equal credit. They were supported by other millions in the armed forces who through no fault of their own could not go overseas and who rendered indispensable service in this country. They were supported by millions in all levels of government, including many volunteers, whose devoted public service furnished basic organization and leadership. They were also supported by the millions of Americans in private life—men and women in industry, in commerce, on the farms, and in all manner of activity on the home front—who contributed their brains and their brawn in arming, equipping, and feeding them. The country was brought through four years of peril by an effort that was truly national in character.

Everlasting tribute and gratitude will be paid by all Americans to those brave men who did not come back, who will never come back—the 330,000 who died that the Nation might live and progress. All Americans will also remain deeply conscious of the obligation owed to that larger number of soldiers, sailors, and marines who suffered wounds and sickness in their service. They may be certain that their sacrifice will never be forgotten or their needs neglected.

The beginning of the year 1946 finds the United States strong and deservedly confident. We have a record of enormous achievements as a democratic society in solving problems and meeting opportunities as they developed. We find ourselves possessed of immeasurable advantages—vast and varied natural resources; great plants, institutions, and other facilities; unsurpassed technological and managerial skills; an alert, resourceful, and able citizenry. We have in the United States Government rich resources in information, perspective, and facilities for doing whatever may be found necessary to do in giving support and form to the widespread and diversified efforts of all our people.

And for the immediate future the business prospects are generally so favorable that there is danger of such feverish and opportunistic activity that our grave postwar problems may be neglected. We need to act now will full regard for pitfalls; we need to act with foresight and balance. We should not be lulled by the immediate alluring prospects into forgetting the fundamental complexity of modern affairs, the catastrophe that can come in this complexity, or the values that can be wrested from it.

But the long-range difficulties we face should no more lead to despair than our immediate business prospects should lead to the optimism which comes from the present short-range prospect. On the foundation of our victory we can build a lasting peace, with greater freedom and security for mankind in our country and throughout the world. We will more certainly do this if we are constantly aware of the fact that we face crucial issues and prepare now to meet them.

To achieve success will require both boldness in setting our sights and caution in steering our way on an uncharted course. But we have no luxury of choice. We must move ahead. No return to the past is possible.

Our Nation has always been a land of great opportunities for those people of the world who sought to become part of us. Now we have become a land of great responsibilities to all the people of all the world. We must squarely recognize and face the fact of those responsibilities. Advances in science, in communication, in transportation, have compressed the world into a community. The economic and political health of each member of the world community bears directly on the economic and political health of each other member.

The evolution of centuries has brought us to a new era in world history in which manifold relationships between nations must be formalized and developed in new and intricate ways.

The United Nations Organization now being established represents a minimum essential beginning. It must be developed rapidly and steadily. It s work must be amplified to fill in the whole pattern that has been out-lined. Economic collaboration, for example, already charted, now must be carried on as carefully and as comprehensively as the political and security measures.

It is important that the nations come together as States in the Assembly and in the Security Council and in the other specialized assemblies and councils that have been and will be arranged. But this is not enough. Our ultimate security requires more than a process of consultation and compromise.

It requires that we begin now to develop the United Nations Organization as the representative of the world as one society. The United Nations Organization, if we have the will adequately to staff it and to make it work as it should, will provide a great voice to speak constantly and responsibly in terms of world collaboration and world well-being.

There are many new responsibilities for us as we enter into this new international era. The whole power and will and wisdom of our Government and of our people should be focused to contribute to and to influence international action. It is intricate, continuing business. Many concessions and adjustments will be required.

The spectacular progress of science in recent years make these necessities more vivid and urgent. That progress has speeded internal development and has changed world relationships so fast that we must realize the fact of a new era. It is an era in which affairs have become complex and rich in promise. Delicate and intricate relationships, involving us all in countless ways, must be carefully considered.

On the domestic scene, as well as on the international scene, we must lay a new and better foundation for cooperation. We face a great peacetime venture; the challenging venture of a free enterprise economy making full and effective use of its rich resources and technical advances. This is a venture in which business, agriculture, and labor have vastly greater opportunities than heretofore. But they all also have vastly greater responsibilities. We will not measure up to those responsibilities by the simple return to "normalcy" that was tried after the last war.

The general objective, on the contrary, is to move forward to find the way in time of peace to the full utilization and development of our physical and human resources that were demonstrated so effectively in the war.

To accomplish this. it is not intended that the Federal Government should do things that can be done as well for the Nation by private enterprise, or by State and local governments. On the contrary, the war has demonstrated how effectively we can organize our productive system and develop the potential abilities of our people by aiding the efforts of private enterprise.

As we move toward one common objective there will be many and urgent problems to meet.

Industrial peace between management and labor will have to be achieved —through the process of collective bargaining—with Government assistance but not Goverment compulsion. This is a problem which is the concern not only of management, labor, and the Government, but also the concern of every one of us.

Private capital and private management are entitled to adequate reward for efficiency, but business must recognize that its reward results from the employment of the resources of the Nation. Business is a public trust and must adhere to national standards in the conduct of its affairs. These standards include as a minimum the establishement of fair wages and fair employment practices.

Labor also has its own new peacetime responsibilities. Under our collective bargaining system, which must become progressively more secure, labor attains increasing political as well as economic power, and this, as with all power, means increased responsibility.

The lives of millions of veterans and war workers will be greatly affected by the success or failure of our program of war liquidation and reconversion. Their transition to peacetime pursuits will be determined by our efforts to break the bottlenecks in key items of production, to make surplus property immediately available where it is needed, to maintain an effective national employment service, and many other reconversion policies. Our obligations to the people who won the war will not be paid if we fail to prevent inflation and to maintain employment opportunities.

While our peacetime prosperity will be based on the private enterprise system, Government can and must assist in many ways. It is the Government's responsibility to see that our economic system remains competitive that new businesses have adequate opportunities, and that our national resources are restored and improved. Government must realize the effect of its operations on the whole economy. It is the responsibility of Government to gear its total program to the achievement of full production and full employment.

Our basic objective—toward which all others lead—is to improve the welfare of the American people. In addition to economic prosperity, this means that we need social security in the fullest sense of the term; the people must be protected from the fear of want during old age, sickness, and unemployment. Opportunities for a good education and adequate medical care must be generally available. Every family should have a decent home. The new economic bill of rights to which I have referred on previous occasions is a charter of economic freedom which seeks to assure that all who will may work toward their own security and the general advancement; that we become a well-housed people, a well-nourished people, an educated people, a people socially and economically secure, an alert and responsible people.

These and other problems which may face us can be met by the cooperation of all of us in furthering a positive and well-balanced Government program—a program which will further national and international well-being. . . .

STATE OF THE UNION MESSAGE
January 6, 1947

In the shortest Annual Message to Congress of his administration, Truman spoke, in general terms, of his projected Fair Deal program for the coming year.

Mr. President, Mr. Speaker, Members of the Congress of the United States:
It looks like a good many of you have moved over to the left since I was here last!

I come before you today to report on the State of the Union and, in the words of the Constitution, to recommend such measures as I judge necessary and expedient.

I come also to welcome you as you take up your duties and to discuss with you the manner in which you and I should fulfill our obligations to the American people during the next 2 years.

The power to mold the future of this Nation lies in our hands—yours and mine, and they are joined together by the Constitution.

If in this year, and in the next, we can find the right course to take as each issue arises, and if, in spite of all difficulties, we have the courage and the resolution to take that course, then we shall achieve a state of well-being for our people without precedent in history. And if we continue to work with the other nations of the world earnestly, patiently, and wisely, we can —granting a will for peace on the part of our neighbors—make a lasting peace for the world.

But, if we are to realize these ends, the Congress and the President, during the next 2 years, must work together. It is not unusual in our history that the majority of the Congress represents a party in opposition to the President's party. I am the twentieth President of the United States who, at some time during his term of office, has found his own party to be in the minority in one or both Houses of Congress. The first one was George Washington. Wilson was number eighteen, and Hoover was number nineteen.

I realize that on some matters the Congress and the President may have honest differences of opinion. Partisan differences, however, did not cause material disagreements as to the conduct of the war. Nor, in the conduct of our international relations, during and since the war, have such partisan differences been material.

On some domestic issues we may, and probably shall, disagree. That in itself is not to be feared. It is inherent in our form of Government. But there are ways of disagreeing; men who differ can still work together sincerely for the common good. We shall be risking the Nation's safety and destroying our opportunities for progress if we do not settle any disagreements in this spirit, without thought of partisan advantage.

THE GENERAL DOMESTIC ECONOMY

As the year 1947 begins, the state of our national economy presents great opportunities for all. We have virtually full employment. Our national production of goods and services is 50 percent higher than in any year prior to the war emergency. The national income in 1946 was higher than in any peacetime year. Our food production is greater than it has ever been. During the last 5 years our productive facilities have been expanded in almost every field. The American standard of living is higher now than ever before, and when the housing shortage can be overcome it will be even higher.

During the past few months we have removed at a rapid rate the emergency controls that the Federal Government had to exercise during the war. The remaining controls will be retained only as long as they are needed to protect the public. Private enterprise must be given the greatest possible freedom to continue the expansion of our economy.

In my proclamation of December 31, 1946, I announced the termination of hostilities. This automatically ended certain temporary legislation and certain executive powers.

Two groups of temporary laws still remain: the first are those which by Congressional mandate are to last during the "emergency"; the second are those which are to continue until the "termination of the war."

I shall submit to the Congress recommendations for the repeal of certain of the statutes which by their terms continue for the duration of the "emergency." I shall at the same time recommend that others within this classification be extended until the state of war has been ended by treaty or by legislative action. As to those statutes which continue until the state of war has been terminated, I urge that the Congress promptly consider each statute individually, and repeal such emergency legislation where it is advisable.

Now that nearly all wartime controls have been removed, the operation of our industrial system depends to a greater extent on the decisions of businessmen, farmers, and workers. These decisions must be wisely made with genuine concern for public welfare. The welfare of businessmen, farmers, and workers depends upon the economic well-being of those who buy their products.

An important present source of danger to our economy is the possibility that prices might be raised to such an extent that the consuming public could not purchase the tremendous volume of goods and services which will be produced during 1947.

We all know that recent price increases have denied to many of our workers much of the value of recent wage increases. Farmers have found that a large part of their increased income has been absorbed by increased prices. While some of our people have received raises in income which exceed prices increases, the great majority have not. Those persons who live on modest fixed incomes—retired persons living on pensions, for example—and workers whose incomes are relatively inflexible, such as teachers and other civil servants—have suffered hardship.

In the effort to bring about a sound and equitable price structure, each group of our population has its own responsibilities.

It is up to industry not only to hold the line on existing prices, but to make reductions whenever profits justify such action.

It is up to labor to refrain from pressing for unjustified wage increases that will force increases in the price level.

And it is up to Government to do everything in its power to encourage high-volume production, for that is what makes possible good wages, low prices, and reasonable profits.

In a few days there will be submitted to the Congress the Economic Report of the President, and also the Budget Message. Those messages will contain many recommendations. Today I shall outline five major economic policies which I believe the Government should pursue during 1947.
These policies are designed to meet our immediate needs and, at the same time, to provide for the long-range welfare of our free enterprise system:

First, the promotion of greater harmony between labor and management.

Second, restriction of monopoly and unfair business practices; assistance to small business; and the promotion of the free competitive system of private enterprise.

Third, continuation of an aggressive program of home construction.

Fourth, the balancing of the budget in the next fiscal year and the achieving of a substantial surplus to be applied to the reduction of the public debt.

Fifth, protection of a fair level of return to farmers in post-war agriculture. . . .

CIVIL RIGHTS

We have recently witnessed in this country numerous attacks upon the constitutional rights of individual citizens as a result of racial and religious bigotry. Substantial segments of our people have been prevented from exercising fully their right to participate in the election of public officials, both locally and nationally. Freedom to engage in lawful callings has been denied.

The will to fight these crimes should be in the hearts of every one of us.

For the Federal Government that fight is now being carried on by the Department of Justice to the full extent of the powers that have been conferred upon it. While the Constitution withholds from the Federal Government the major task of preserving peace in the several States, I am not convinced that the present legislation reached the limit of Federal power to protect the civil rights of its citizens.

I have, therefore, by Executive order, established the President's Committee on Civil Rights to study and report on the whole problem of federally-secured civil rights, with a view to making recommendations to the Congress . . . .

FOREIGN AFFAIRS

Progress in reaching our domestic goals is closely related to our conduct of foreign affairs. All that I have said about maintaining a sound and prosperous economy and improving the welfare of our people has greater meaning because of the world leadership of the United States. What we do, or fail to do, at home affects not only ourselves but millions throughout the world. If we are to fulfill our responsibilities to ourselves and to other peoples, we must make sure that the United States is sound economically, socially, and politically. Only then will we be able to help bring about the elements of peace in other countries—political stability, economic advancement, and social progress.

Peace treaties for Italy, Bulgaria, Rumania, and Hungary have finally been prepared. Following the signing of these treaties next month in Paris, they will be submitted to the Senate for ratification. This Government does not regard the treaties as completely satisfactory. Whatever their defects, however, I am convinced that they are as good as we can hope to obtain by agreement among the principal wartime Allies. Further dispute and delay would gravely jeopardize political stability in the countries concerned for many years.

During the long months of debate on these treaties, we have made it clear to all nations that the United States will not consent to settlements at the expense of principles we regard as vital to a just and enduring peace. We have made it equally clear that we will not retreat to isolationism. Our policies will be the same during the forthcoming negotiations in Moscow on the German and Austrian treaties, and during the future conferences on the Japanese treaty.

The delay in arriving at the first peace settlements is due partly to the difficulty of reaching agreement with the Soviet Union on the terms of settlement. Whatever differences there may have been between us and the Soviet Union, however, should not be allowed to obscure the fact that the basic interests of both nations lie in the early making of a peace under which the peoples of all countries may return, as free men and women, to the essential taks of production and reconstruction. The major concern of each of us should be the promotion of collective security, not the advancement of individual security.

Our policy toward the Soviet Union is guided by the same principles which determine our policies toward all nations. We seek only to uphold the principles of international justice which have been embodied in the Charter of the United Nations.

We must now get on with the peace settlements. The occupying powers should recognize the independence of Austria and withdraw their troops. The Germans and the Japanese cannot be left in doubt and fear as to their future; they must know their national boundaries, their resources, and what reparations they must pay. Without trying to manage their internal affairs, we can insure that these countries do not re-arm.

INTERNATIONAL RELIEF AND DISPLACED PERSONS

The United States can be proud of its part in caring for the peoples reduced to want by the ravages of war, and in aiding nations to restore their national economies. We have shipped more supplies to the hungry peoples of the world since the end of the war than all other countries combined!

However, insofar as admitting displaced persons is concerned, I do not feel that the United States had done its part. Only about 5,000 of them have entered this country since May, 1946. The fact is that the executive agencies are now doing all that is reasonably possible under the limitations of the existing law and established quotas. Congressional assistance in the form of new legislation is needed. I urge the Congress to turn its attention to this world problem, in an effort to find ways whereby we can fulfill our responsibilities to these thousands of homeless and suffering refugees of all faith. . .

ATOMIC ENERGY

The United States has taken the lead in the endeavor to put atomic energy under effective international control. We seek no monopoly for ourselves or for any group of nations. We ask only that there be safeguards sufficient to insure that no nation will be able to use this power for military purposes. So long as all governments are not agreed on means of international control of atomic energy, the shadow of fear will obscure the bright prospects for the peaceful use of this enormous power.

In accordance with the Atomic Energy Act of 1946, the Commission established under that law is assuming full jurisdiction over domestic atomic energy enterprise. The program of the Commission will, of course, be worked out in close collaboration with the military services in conformity with the wish of the Congress, but it is my fervent hope that the military significance of atomic energy will steadily decline. We look to the Commission to foster the development of atomic energy for industrial use and scientific and medical research. In the vigorous and effective development of peaceful uses of atomic energy rests our hope that this new force may ultimately be turned into a blessing . . .

THE TRUMAN DOCTRINE
March 12, 1947

The basic idea of this message, was that the United States was to underwrite the defense of free states against totalitarian regimes. It was widely hailed as a sharp new turn in American Foreign policy.

The gravity of the situation which confronts the world today necessitates my appearance before a joint session of the Congress. The foreign policy and the national security of this country are involved.

One aspect of the present situation, which I wish to present to you at this time for your consideration and decision, concerns Greece and Turkey.

The United States has received from the Greek Government an urgent appeal for financial and economic assistance. Preliminary reports from the American Economic Mission now in Greece and reports from the American Ambassador in Greece corroborate the statement of the Greek Government that assistance is imperative if Greece is to survive as a free nation.

I do not believe that the American people and the Congress wish to turn a deaf ear to the appeal of the Greek Government.

The very existence of the Greek state is today threatened by the terrorists activities of several thousand armed men, led by Communists, who defy the Government's authority at a number of points, particularly along the northern boundaries. A commission appointed by the United Nations Security Council is at present investigating disturbed conditions in Northern Greece and alleged border violations along the frontiers between Greece on the one hand and Albania, Bulgaria and Yugoslavia on the other.

Meanwhile, the Greek Government is unable to cope with the situation. The Greek Army is small and poorly equipped. It needs supplies and equipment if it is to restore the authority to the Government throughout Greek territory.

Greece must have assistance if it is to become a self-supporting and self-respecting democracy. The United States must supply this assistance. We have already extended to Greece certain types of relief and economic aid but these are inadequate. There is no other country to which democratic Greece can turn. No other nation is willing and able to provide necessary support for a democratic Greek Government.

The British Government, which has been helping Greece, can give no further financial or economic aid after March 31. Great Britain finds itself under the necessity of reducing or liquidating its committments in several parts of the world, including Greece.

We have considered how the United Nations might assist in this crisis. But the situation is an urgent one requiring immediate action, and the United

Nations and its related organizations are not in a position to extend help of the kind that is required. . . .

Greece's neighbor, Turkey, also deserves our attention. The future of Turkey as an independent and economically sound state is clearly no less important to the freedom-loving peoples of the world than the future of Greece. The circumstances in which Turkey finds itself today are considerably different from those of Greece. Turkey has been spared the disasters that have beset Greece. And during the war, the United States and Great Britain furnished Turkey with material aid. Nevertheless, Turkey now needs our support.

Since the war Turkey has sought additional financial assistance from Great Britain and the United States for the purpose of effecting the modernization necessary for the maintenance of its national integrity. That integrity is essential to the preservation of order in the Middle East.

The British Government has informed us that, owning to its own difficulties, is can no longer extend financial or economic aid to Turkey. As in the case of Greece, if Turkey is to have the assistance it needs, the United States must supply it. We are the only country able to provide that help.

I am fully aware of the broad implications involved if the United States extends assistance to Greece and Turkey, and I shall discuss these implications with you at this time.

One of the primary objectives of the foreign policy of the United States is the creation of conditions in which we and other nations will be able to work out a way of life free from coercion. This was a fundamental issue in the war with Germany and Japan. Our victory was won over countries which sought to impose their will, and their way of life, upon other nations.

To ensure the peaceful development of nations, free from coercion, the United States has taken a leading part in establishing the United Nations. The United Nations is designed to make possible lasting freedom and independence for all its members. We shall not realize our objectives, however, unless we are willing to help free peoples to maintain their free institutions and their national integrity against aggressive movements that seek to impose on them totalitarian regimes. This is no more than a frank recognition that totalitarian regimes imposed on free peoples, by direct or indirect aggression, undermine the foundations of international peace and hence the secruity of the United States.

The peoples of a number of countries of the world have recently had totalitarian regimes forced upon them against their will. The Government of the United States has made frequent protests against coercion and intimidation, in violation of the Yalta Agreement, in Poland, Rumania and Bulgaria. I must also state that in a number of other countries there have been similar developments.

At the present moment in world history nearly every nation must choose between alternative ways of life. The choice is too often not a free one.

One way of life is based upon the will of the majority, and is distinguished by free institutions, representative government, free elections, guarantees of individual liberty, freedom of speech and religion, and freedom from political oppression.

The second way of life is based upon the will of the minority forcibly imposed upon the majority. It relies upon terror and oppression, a controlled press and radio, fixed elections, and the suppression of personal freedoms.

I believe that it must be the policy of the United States to support free peoples who are resisting attempted subjugation by armed minorities or by outside pressures.

I believe that we must assist free peoples to work out their own destinies in their own way.

I believe that our help should be primarily through economic and financial aid which is essential to economic stability and orderly political processes.

The world is not static, and the status quo is not sacred. But we cannot allow changes in the status quo in violation of the charter of the United Nations by such methods as coercion, or by such subterfuges as political infiltration. In helping free and independent nations to maintain their freedom, the United States will be giving effect to the principles of the charter of the United Nations.

It is necessary only to glance at a map to realize that the survival and integrity of the Greek nation are of grave importance in a much wider situation. If Greece should fall under the control of an armed minority, the effect upon its neighbor, Turkey, would be immediate and serious. Confusion and disorder might well spread throughout the entire Middle East.

Moreover, the disappearance of Greece as an independent state would have a profound effect upon those countries in Europe whose peoples are struggling against great difficulties to maintain their freedoms and their independence while they repair the damages of war.

It would be an unspeakable tragedy if these countries, which have struggled so long against overwhelming odds, should lose that victory for which they sacrificed so much. Collapse of free institutions and loss of independence would be disastrous not only for them but for the world. Discouragement and possibly failure would quickly be the lot of neighboring peoples striving to maintain their freedom and independence.

Should we fail to aid Greece and Turkey in this fateful hour, the effect will be far reaching to the west as well as to the east. We must take immediate and resolute action.

I therefore ask the Congress to provide authority for assistance to Greece and Turkey in the amount of $400,000,000 for the period ending June 30, 1948.

In addition to funds, I ask the Congress to authorize the detail of American civilian and military personnel to Greece and Turkey, at the request of those countries, to assist in the tasks of reconstruction, and for the purpose of supervising the use of such financial and material assistance as may be furnished. I recommend that authority also be provided for the instruction and training of selected Greek and Turkish personnel.

Finally, I ask that the Congress provide authority which will permit the speediest and most effective use, in terms of needed commodities, supplies, and equipment, of such funds as may be authorized. . . .

The seeds of totalitarian regimes are nurtured by misery and want. They spread and grow in the evil soil of poverty and strife. They reach their full growth when the hope of a people for a better life has died. We must keep that hope alive. The free peoples of the world look to us for support in maintaining their freedoms.

If we falter in our leadership, we may endanger the peace of the world—and we shall surely endanger the welfare of this nation.

Great responsibilities have been placed upon us by the swift movement of events. I am confident that the Congress will face these responsibilities squarely.

TRUMAN LOYALTY ORDER
March 22, 1947

As the cold war grew more intense, Truman believed that some sort of program for combatting subversion within the government was necessary. These are the details of that program.

PART I

INVESTIGATION OF APPLICANTS

1. There shall be a loyalty investigation of every person entering the civilian employment of any department or agency of the Executive Branch of the Federal Government.

A. Investigations of persons entering the competitive service shall be conducted by the Civil Service Commission, except in such cases as are covered by a special agreement between the commission and any given department or agency.

B. Investigations of persons other than those entering the competitive service shall be conducted by the employing department or agency. Departments and agencies without investigative organizations shall utilize the investigative facilities of the Civil Service Commission.

2. The investigations of persons entering the employ of the Executive Branch may be conducted after any such person enters upon actual employment therein, but in any such case the appointment of such person shall be conditioned upon a favorable determination with respect to his loyalty. . . .

3. An investigation shall be made of all applicants at all available pertinent sources of information and shall include reference to:

A. Federal Bureau of Investigation files.

B. Civil Service Commission files.

C. Military and Naval Intelligence files.

D. The files of any other appropriate government investigative or intelligence agency.

E. House Committee on un-American Activities files.

F. Local law-enforcement files at the place of residence and employment of the applicant, including municipal, county and state law-enforcement files.

G. Schools and colleges attended by applicant.

H. Former employers of applicant.

I. References given by applicant.

J. Any other appropriate source.

4. Whenever derogatory information with respect to loyalty of an appli-

cant is revealed, a full field investigation shall be conducted. A full field investigation shall also be conducted of those applicants, or of any applicants for particular positions, as may be designated by the head of the employing department or agency, such designations to be based on the determination by any such head of the best interests of national security.

VETO OF TAFT-HARTLEY BILL
June 20, 1947

*Nothing did more to win for Truman the gratitude and support
of organized Labor than the veto of this bill. It was eventually
passed over his veto.*

. . .I find that this bill is completely contrary to that national policy of
economic freedom. It would require the Government, in effect, to become
an unwanted participant at every bargaining table. It would establish by
law limitations on the terms of every bargaining agreement, and nullify
thousands of agreements mutually arrived at and satisfactory to the parties.
It would inject the Government deeply into the process by which employers
and workers reach agreement. It would superimpose bureaucratic procedures on the free decisions of local employers and employees.

At a time when we are determined to remove, as rapidly as practicable,
Federal controls established during the war, this bill would involve the
Government in free processes of our economic system to a degree unpre-
cedented in peacetime. . . .

The bill prescribes unequal penalties for the same offense. It would require
the National Labor Relations Board to give priority to charges against
workers over related charges against employers. It would discriminate
against workers by arbitrarily penalizing them for all critical strikes.

Much has been made of the claim that the bill is intended simply to
equalize the positions of labor and management. Careful analysis shows
that this claim is unfounded. Many of the provisions of the bill standing alone
seem innocent but, considered in relation to each other, reveal a consistent
pattern of inequality. . . .

4. *The bill would deprive workers of vital protection which they now have
   under the law*

(1) The bill would make it easier for an employer to get rid of employees
whom he wanted to discharge because they exercised their right of self-
organization guaranteed by the act. It would permit an employer to dismiss
a man on the pretext of a slight infraction of shop rules, even though his real
motive was to discriminate against this employee for union activity.

(2) The bill would also put a powerful new weapon in the hands of
employers by permitting them to initiate elections at times strategically
advantageous to them. It is significant that employees on economic strike
who may have been replaced are denied a vote. An employer could easily
thwart the will of his employees by raising a question of representation at a
time when the union was striking over contract terms.

(3) It would give employers the means to engage in endless litigation,
draining the energy and resources of unions in court actions, even though

the particular charges were groundless.

(4) It would deprive workers of the power to meet the competition of goods produced under sweatshop conditions by permitting employers to halt every type of secondary boycott, not merely those for unjustifiable purposes.

(5) It would reduce the responsibility of employers for unfair labor practices committed in their behalf. The effect of the bill is to narrow unfairly employer liability for antiunion acts and statements made by persons who, in the eyes of the employees affected, act and speak for management, but who may be "agents' in the strict legal sense of that term.

(6) At the same time it would expose unions to suits for acts of violence, wildcat strikes and other actions, none of which were authorized or ratified by them. By employing elaborate legal doctrine, the bill applies a superficially superior test of responsibility for employers and unions—each would be responsible for the acts of his "agents." But the power of an employer to control the acts of his subordinates is direct and final. This is radically different from the power of unions to control the acts of their members— who are, after all, members of a free association. . . .

6. *The bill would establish an ineffective and discriminatory emergency procedure for dealing with major strikes affecting the public health or safety*

This procedure would be certain to do more harm than good, and to increase rather than diminish widespread industrial disturbances. Its essential features are a Presidential board of inquiry, a waiting period of approximately 80 days (enforced by injunction), and a secret ballot vote of the workers on the question of whether or not to accept their employer's last offer. . . .

After this elaborate procedue the injunction would then have to be dissolved, the parties would be free to fight out their dispute, and it would be mandatory for the President to transfer the whole problem to the Congress, even if it were not in session. Thus, major economic disputes between employers and their workers over contract terms might ultimately be thrown into the political arena for disposition. One could scarcely devise a less effective method for discouraging critical strikes.

This entire procedure is based upon the same erroneous assumptions as those which underlay the strike-vote provision of the War Labor Disputes Act, namely, that strikes are called in haste as the result of inflamed passions, and that union leaders do not represent the wishes of the workers. We have learned by experience, however, that strikes in the basic industries are not called in haste, but only after long periods of negotiation and serious deliberation; and that in the secret-ballot election the workers almost always vote to support their leaders.

Furthermore, a fundamental inequity runs through these provisions.

The bill provides for injunctions to prohibit workers from striking, even against terms dictated by employers after contracts have expired. There is no provision assuring the protection of the rights of the employees during the period they are deprived of the right to protect themselves by economic action. . . .

9. *The bill raises serious issues of public policy which transcend labor-management difficulties*

(1) In undertaking to restrict political contributions and expenditures, the bill would prohibit many legitimate activities on the part of unions and corporations. This provision would prevent the ordinary union newspaper from commenting favorably or unfavorably upon candidates or issues in national elections. I regard this as a dangerous intrusion on free speech, unwarranted by any demonstration of need, and quite foreign to the stated purposes of this bill.

Furthermore, this provision can be interpreted as going far beyond its apparent objectives, and as interfering with necessary business activities. It provides no exemption for corporations whose business is the publication of newspapers or the operation of radio stations. It makes no distinctions between expenditures made by such corporations for the purpose of influencing the results of an election, and other expenditures made by them in the normal course of their business "in connection with" an election. Thus it would raise a host of troublesome questions concerning the legality of many practices ordinarily engaged in by newspapers and radio stations.

(2) In addition, in one important area the bill expressly abandons the principle of uniform application of national policy under Federal law. The bill's stated policy of preserving some degree of union security would be abdicated in all States where more restrictive policies exist. In other respects the bill makes clear that Federal policy would govern insofar as activities affecting commerce are concerned. This is not only an invitation to the States to distort national policy as they see fit, but is a complete forsaking of a long-standing constitutional principle.

(3) In regard to Communists in unions, I am convinced that the bill would have an effect exactly opposite to that intended by the Congress. Congress intended to assist labor organizations to rid themselves of Communist officers. With this objective I am in full accord. But the effect of this provision would be far different. The bill would deny the peaceful procedures of the National Labor Relations Act to a union unless all its officers declared under oath that they were not members of the Communist Party and that they did not favor the forceful or unconstitutional overthrow of the Government. The mere refusal by a single individual to sign the required affidavit would prevent an entire national labor union from being certified for purposes of collective bargaining. Such a union would have to win all its objectives by strike, rather than by orderly procedure

under the law. The union and the affected industry would be disrupted for perhaps a long period of time while violent electioneering, charges and countercharges split open the union ranks. The only result of this provision would be confusion and disorder, which is exactly the result the Communists desire.

This provision in the bill is an attempt to solve difficult problems of industrial democracy by recourse to oversimplified legal devices. I consider that this provision would increase, rather than decrease, disruptive effects of Communists in our labor movement.

The most fundamental test which I have applied to this bill is whether it would strengthen or weaken American democracy in the present critical hour. This bill is perhaps the most serious economic and social legislation of the past decade. Its effects—for good or ill—would be felt for decades to come.

I have concluded that the bill is a clear threat to the successful working of our democratic society.

One of the major lessons of recent world history is that free and vital trade unions are a strong bulwark against the growth of totalitarian movements. We must, therefore, be everlastingly alert that in striking at union abuses we do not destroy the contribution which unions make to our democratic strength.

This bill would go far toward weakening our trade-union movement. And it would go far toward destroying our national unity. By raising barriers between labor and management and by injecting political considerations into normal economic decisions, it would invite them to gain their ends through direct political action. I think it would be exceedingly dangerous to our country to develop a class basis for political action.

STATE OF THE UNION MESSAGE
January 8, 1948

While this message reflects the President's great concern with international affairs and the cold war, it, nevertheless, places especial emphasis on improvements in civil rights, social security and education.

I sincerely hope that all of you had a pleasant holiday season and that you won't have too much hard work in the coming year.

Mr. President, Mr. Speaker and members of the Eightieth Congress:

We are here today to consider the state of the Union.

On this occasion, above all others, the Congress and the President should concentrate their attention, not upon party, but upon the country; not upon the things which divide us but upon those which bind us together—the enduring principles of our American system, and our common aspirations for the future welfare and security of the United States. . . .

Our First Goal Defined

Our first goal is to secure fully the essential human rights of our citizens.

The United States has always had a deep concern for human rights. Religious freedom, free speech and freedom of thought are cherished realities in our land. Any denial of human rights is a denial of the basic beliefs of democracy and of our regard for the worth of each individual.

Today, however, some of our citizens are still denied equal opportunity for education, for jobs and economic advancement, and for the expression of their views at the polls. Most serious of all, some are denied equal protection under the laws. Whether discrimination is based on race, or creed, or color, or land or origin, it is utterly contrary to American ideas of democracy.

The recent report of the President's Committee on Civil Rights points the way to corrective action by the Federal Government and by state and local governments. Because of the need for effective Federal action, I shall send a special message to the Congress on this important subject.

We should also consider our obligations to assure the fullest possible measure of civil rights to the people of our territories and possessions. I believe that the time has come for Alaska and Hawaii to be admitted to the Union as states.

Our second goal is to protect and develop our human resources.

The safeguarding of the rights of our citizens must be accompanied by an equal regard for their opportunities for development and their protection from economic insecurity. In this nation the ideas of freedom and equality can be given specific meaning in terms of health, education, social security and housing.

Over the past twelve years we have erected a sound framework of social security legislation. Many millions of our citizens are now protected against the loss of income which can come with unemployment, old-age, or the death of wage-earners. Yet our system has gaps and inconsistencies; it is only half-finished.

We should now extend unemployment compensation, old-age benefits and survivors' benefits to millions who are not now protected. We should also raise the level of benefits.

The greatest gap in our Social Security structure is the lack of adequate provision for the nation's health. We are rightly proud of the high standards of medical care we know how to provide in the United States. The fact is, however, that most of our people cannot afford to pay for the care they need.

I have often and strongly urged that this condition demands a national health program. The heart of the program must be a national system of payment for medical care based on well-tried insurance principles. This great nation cannot afford to allow its citizens to suffer needlessly from the lack of proper medical care.

Our ultimate aim must be a comprehensive insurance system to protect all our people equally against insecurity and ill-health.

Another fundamental aim of our democracy is to provide an adequate education for every person.

Our educational systems face a financial crisis. It is deplorable that in a nation as rich as ours there are millions of children who do not have adequate schoolhouses or enough teachers for a good elementary or secondary education. If there are educational inadequacies in any state the whole nation suffers. The Federal Government has a responsibility for providing financial aid to meet this crisis.

Requirements of Democracy

In addition, we must make possible greater equality of opportunity to all our citizens for an education. Only by so doing can we insure that our citizens will be capable of understanding and sharing the responsibilities of democracy.

The Government's program for health, education and security are of such great importance to our democracy that we should now establish an executive department for their administration.

Health and education have their beginning in the home. No matter what our hospitals or schools are like, the youth of our nation are handicapped when millions of them live in city slums and country shacks. Within the next decade we must see that every American family has a decent home.

As an immediate step we need the long-range housing program which I have recommended on many occasions to this Congress. This should include financial aids designed to yield more housing at lower prices. It should provide public housing for low-income families, and vigorous development of new techniques to lower the cost of building.

Until we can overcome the present drastic housing shortage we must extend and strengthen rent control.

We have had, and shall continue to have, a special interest in the welfare of our veterans. Over 14 million men and women who served in the armed forces in World War II have now returned to civilian life. Over two million veterans are being helped through school. Millions have been aided while finding jobs, and have been helped in buying homes, in obtaining medical care, and in adjusting themselves to physical handicaps.

All but a very few veterans have successfully made the transition from military life to their home communities. The success of our veterans' program is proved by this fact. This nation is proud of the eagerness shown by our veterans to become self-reliant and self-supporting citizens. . . .

Our Policies for Peace

For these reasons the United States is vigorously following policies designed to achieve a peaceful and prosperous world.

We are giving, and will continue to give, our full support to the United Nations. While that organization has encountered unforeseen and unwelcome difficulties, I am confident of its ultimate success. We are also devoting our efforts toward world economic recovery and the revival of world trade. These actions are closely related and mutually supporting.

We believe that the United States can be an effective force for world peace only if it is strong. We look forward to the day when nations will decrease their armaments. Yet so long as there remains serious opposition to the ideals of a peaceful world, we must maintain strong armed forces.

The passage of the National Security Act by the Congress at its last session was a notable step in providing for the security of this country. A further step which I consider of even greater importance is the early provision for universal training. There are many elements in a balanced national security program, all interrelated and necessary, but universal training should be the foundation for them all. A favorable decision by the Congress at an early date is of world importance. I am convinced that such action is vital to the security of this nation and to the maintenance of its leadership.

The United States is engaged today in many international activities directed toward the creation of lasting peaceful relationships among nations.

We have been giving substantial aid to Greece and Turkey to assist these nations in preserving their integrity against foreign pressures. Had it not been for our aid, their situation today might well be radically different. . . .

Many thousands of displaced persons, still living in camps overseas, should be allowed entry into the United States. I again urge the Congress to pass suitable legislation at once so that this nation may do its share in caring for the homeless and suffering refugees of all faiths. I believe that the admission of these persons will add to the strength and energy of this nation.

We are moving toward our goal of world peace in many ways. But the most important effort which we are now making are those which support world economic reconstruction. We are seeking to restore the world trading system which was shattered by the war and to remedy the economic paralysis which grips many countries.

To restore world trade we have recently taken the lead in bringing about the greatest reduction of world tariffs that the world has ever seen. The extension of the provisions of the Reciprocal Trade Agreements Act, which made this achievement possible, is of extreme importance. We must also go on to support the International Trade Organization, through which we hope to obtain world-wide agreement on a code of fair conduct in international trade.

Our present major effort toward economic reconstruction is to support the program for recovery developed by the countries of Europe. In my recent message to the Congress I outlined the reasons why it is wise and necessary for the United States to extend this support.

I want to reaffirm my belief in the soundness and promise of this proposal. When the European economy is strengthened, the product of its industry will be of benefit to many other areas of economic distress. The ability of free men to overcome hunger and despair will be a moral stimulus to the entire world. . . .

We are building toward a world where all nations, large and small alike, may live free from the fear of aggression.

This leads to peace—not war.

Above all else, we are striving to achieve a concord among the peoples of the world based upon the individual and the brotherhood of man.

This leads to peace—not war.

We can go forward with confidence that we are following sound policies, both at home and with other nations, which will lead us toward our great goals for economic, social and moral achievement.

As we enter the new year, we must surmount one major problem which affects all our goals. That is the problem of inflation.

Already inflation in this country is undermining the living standards of millions of families. Food costs too much. Housing has reached fantastic price levels. Schools and hospitals are in financial distress. Inflation threatens to bring on disagreement and strife between labor and management.

Worst of all, inflation holds the threat of another depression, just as we had a depression after the unstable boom following the first World War . . .

When we have conquered inflation we shall be in a position to move forward toward our chosen goals.

As we do so let us keep ever before us our high purposes.

We are determined that every citizen of this nation shall have an equal right and an equal opportunity to grow in wisdom and in stature to take his place in the control of his nation's destiny.

We are determined that the productive resources of this nation shall be used wisely and fully for the benefit of all.

We are determined that the democratic faith of our people and the strength of our resources shall contribute their full share to the attainment of an enduring peace in the world.

It is our faith in human dignity that underlies these purposes. It is this faith that keeps us a strong and vital people.

This is a time to remind ourselves of these fundamentals. For today the whole world looks to us for leadership.

This is the hour to rededicate ourselves to the faith in mankind that makes us strong.

This is the time to rededicate ourselves to the faith in God that gives us confidence as we face the challenge of the years ahead.

TRUMAN'S CIVIL RIGHTS MESSAGE
February 2, 1948

Truman called on Congress to implement the program of civil rights proposed by his Committee on Civil Rights. Although this message produced little in the form of new legislation, it did dramatize existing inequities.

To the Congress of the United States:

In the state of the Union message on January 7, 1948, I spoke of five great goals toward which we should strive in our constant effort to strengthen our democracy and improve the welfare of our people. The first of these is to secure fully our essential human rights. I am now presenting to the Congress my recommendations for legislation to carry us forward toward that goal.

This Nation was founded by men and women who sought these shores that they might enjoy greater freedom and greater opportunity than they had known before. The founders of the United States proclaimed to the world the American belief that all men are created equal, and that governments are instituted to secure the inalienable rights with which all men are endowed. In the Declaration of Independence and the Constitution of the United States they eloquently expressed the aspirations of all mankind for equality and freedom.

These ideals inspired the peoples of other lands, and their practical fulfillment made the United States the hope of the oppressed everywhere. Throughout our history men and women of all colors and creeds, of all races and religions, have come to this country to escape tyranny and discrimination. Millions strong, they have helped build this democratic Nation and have constantly reinforced our devotion to the great ideals of liberty and equality. With those who preceded them they have helped to fashion and strengthen our American faith—a faith that can be simply stated:

We believe that all men are created equal and that they have the right to equal justice under law.

We believe that all men have the right to freedom of thought and of expression and the right to worship as they please.

We believe that all men are entitled to equal opportunities for jobs, for for homes, for good health, and for education.

We believe that all men should have a voice in their government, and that government should protect, not usurp, the rights of the people.

These are the basic civil rights which are the source and the support of our democracy.

Today the American people enjoy more freedom and opportunity than ever before. Never in our history has there been better reason to hope for the complete realization of the ideals of liberty and equality.

We shall not, however, finally achieve the ideals for which this Nation was founded so long as any American suffers discrimination as a result of his race, or religion, or color, or the land of origin of his forefathers.

Unfortunately there still are examples—flagrant examples—of discrimination which are utterly contrary to our ideals. Not all groups of our population are free from the fear of violence. Not all groups are free to live and work where they please or to improve their conditions of life by their own efforts. Not all groups enjoy the full privileges of citizenship and participation in the Government under which they live.

We cannot be satisfied until all our people have equal opportunities for jobs, for homes, for education, for health, and for political expression and until all our people have equal protection under the law. . . .

The protection of civil rights is the duty of every government which derives its powers from the consent of the people. This is equally true of local, State, and National Governments. There is much that the States can and should do at this time to extend their protection of civil rights. Wherever the law-enforcement measures of State and local governments are inadequate to discharge this primary function of government, these measures should be strengthened and improved.

The Federal Government has a clear duty to see that constitutional guaranties of individual liberties and of equal protection under the laws are not denied or abridged anywhere in our Union. That duty is shared by all three branches of the Government, but it can be fulfilled only if the Congress enacts modern, comprehensive civil-rights laws, adequate to the needs of the day, and demonstrating our continuing faith in the free way of life.

I recommend, therefore, that the Congress enact legislation at this session directed toward the following specific objectives:

(1) Establishing a permanent Commission on Civil Rights, a Joint Congressional Committee on Civil Rights, and a Civil Rights Division in the Department of Justice.

(2) Strengthening existing civil-rights statutes.

(3) Providing Federal protection against lynching.

(4) Protecting more adequately the right to vote.

(5) Establishing a Fair Employment Practice Commission to prevent unfair discrimination in employment.

(6) Prohibiting discrimination in interstate transportation facilities.

(7) Providing home rule and suffrage in Presidential elections for the residents of the District of Columbia.

(8) Providing statehood for Hawaii and Alaska and a greater measure of self-government for our island possessions.

(9) Equalizing the opportunities for residents of the United States to become naturalized citizens.

(10) Settling the evacuation claims of Japanese-Americans. . . .

The legislation I have recommended for enactment by the Congress at the present session is a minimum program if the Federal Government is to fulfill its obligation of insuring the Constitutional guaranties of individual liberties and of equal protection under the law.

Under the authority of existing law the executive branch is taking every possible action to improve the enforcement of the civil-rights statutes and to eliminate discrimination in Federal employment, in providing Federal services and facilities, and in the armed forces.

I have already referred to the establishment of the Civil Rights Division of the Department of Justice. The Federal Bureau of Investigation will work closely with this new Division in the investigation of Federal civil-rights cases. Specialized training is being given to the Bureau's agents so that they may render more effective service in this difficult field of law enforcement.

It is the settled policy of the United States Government that there shall be no discrimination in Federal employment or in providing Federal services and facilities. Steady progress has been made toward this objective in recent years. I shall shortly issue an Executive order containing an comprehensive restatement of the Federal nondiscrimination policy, together with appropriate measures to ensure compliance.

During the recent war and in the years since its close we have made such progress toward equality of opportunity in our armed services without regard to race, color, religion, or national origin. I have instructed the Secretary of Defense to take steps to have the remaining instances of discrimination in the armed services eliminated as rapidly as possible. The personnel policies and practices of all the services in this regard will be made consistent.

I have instructed the Secretary of the Army to investigate the status of civil rights in the Panama Canal Zone with a view to eliminating such discrimination as may exist there. If legislation is necessary, I shall make appropriate recommendations to the Congress. . . .

The position of the United States in the world today makes it especially urgent that we adopt these measures to secure for all our people their essential rights.

The peoples of the world are faced with the choice of freedom or enslavement, a choice between a form of government which harnesses the state in the service of the individual and a form of government which chains the individual to the needs of the state.

We in the United States are working in company with other nations who share our desire for enduring world peace and who believe with us that, above all else, men must be free. We are striving to build a world family of nations—a world where men may live under governments of their own choosing and under laws of their own making.

As part of that endeavor, the Commission on Human Rights of the United Nations is now engaged in preparing an international bill of human rights by which the nations of the world may bind themselves by internnational covenant to give effect to basic human rights and fundamental freedoms. We have played a leading role in this undertaking designed to create a world order of law and justice fully protective of the rights and the dignity of the individual.

To be effective in these efforts, we must protect our civil rights so that by providing all our people with the maximum enjoyment of personal freedom and personal opportunity we shall be a stronger nation—stronger in our leadership, stronger in our moral position, stronger in the deeper satisfactions of a united citizenry.

We know that our democracy is not perfect. But we do know that it offers a fuller, freer, happier life to our people than any totalitarian nation has ever offered.

If we wish to inspire the peoples of the world whose freedom is in jeopardy, if we wish to restore hope to those who have already lost their civil liberties, if we wish to fulfill the promise that is ours, we must correct the remaining imperfections in our practice of democracy.

We know the way. We need only the will.

HARRY S TRUMAN

STATE OF THE UNION MESSAGE
January 15, 1949

In 1948, the Republicans failed to capture the Presidency. Now President in his own right, Truman put forward a legislative program under a label of his own, the "Fair Deal."

Mr. President, Mr. Speaker, Members of the Congress:

I am happy to report to this Eighty-first Congress that the state of the union is good. Our nation is better able than ever before to meet the needs of the American people, and to give them their fair chance in the pursuit of happiness. This great Republic is foremost among the nations of the world in the search for peace.

During the last sixteen years the American people have been creating a society which offers new opportunities for every man to enjoy his share of the good things of life.

In this society we are conservative about the values and principles which we cherish; but we are forward-looking in protecting those values and principles and in extending their benefits. We have rejected the discredited theory that the fortunes of the nation should be in the hands of a privileged few. We have abandoned the "trickle-down" concept of national prosperity.

Instead, we believe that our economic system should rest on a democratic foundation and that wealth should be created for the benefit of all.

The recent election shows that the people of the United States are in favor of this kind of society and want to go on improving it.

The American people have decided that poverty is just as wasteful and just as unnecessary as preventable disease. We have pledged our common resources to help one another in the hazards and struggles of individual life. We believe that no unfair prejudice or artificial distinction should bar any citizen of the United States of American from an education, or from good health, or from a job that he is capable of performing.

The attainment of this kind of society demands the best efforts of every citizen in every walk of life, and it imposes increasing responsibilities on the Government.

The Government must work with industry, labor and the farmers in keeping our economy running at full speed. The Government must see that every American has a chance to obtain his fair share of our increasing abundance. These responsibilities go hand in hand.

We cannot maintain prosperity unless we have a fair distribution of opportunity and a widespread consumption of the products of our factories and farms.

Our Government has undertaken to meet these responsibilities.

We have made tremendous public investments in highways, hydroelectric power projects, soil conservation and reclamation. We have established a system of social security. We have enacted laws protecting the rights and the welfare of our working people and the income of our farmers.

These Federal policies have paid for themselves many times over. They have strengthened the material foundations of our democratic ideals. Without them our present prosperity would be impossible.

Reinforced by these policies, our private enterprise system has reached new heights of production. Since the boom year of 1929, while our population has increased by only 20 per cent, our agricultural production has increased by 45 per cent, and our industrial production has increased by 75 per cent. We are turning out far more goods and more wealth per worker than we have ever done before.

This progress has confounded the gloomy prophets—at home and abroad —who predicted the downfall of American capitalism. The people of the United States, going their own way, confident in their own powers, have achieved the greatest prosperity the world has ever seen.

But, great as our progress has been, we still have a long way to go.

As we look around the country many of our shortcomings stand out in bold relief.

We are suffering from excessively high prices.

Our production is still not large enough to satisfy our demands.

Our minimum wages are far too low.

Small business is losing ground to growing monopoly.

Our farmers still face an uncertain future. And too many of them lack the benefits of our modern civilization.

Some of our natural resources are still being wasted.

We are acutely short of electric power, although the means for developing such power are abundant.

Five million families are still living in slums and firetraps. Three million families share their homes with others.

Our health is far behind the progress of medical science. Proper medical care is so expensive that it is out of reach of the great majority of our citizens.

Our schools, in many localities, are utterly inadequate.

Our democratic ideals are often thwarted by prejudice and intolerance.

Each of these shortcomings is also an opportunity—an opportunity for the Congress and the President to work for the good of the people.

Our first great opportunity is to protect our economy against the evils of "boom or bust."

This objective cannot be attained by Government alone. Indeed, the greater part of the task must be performed by individual efforts under our system of free enterprise. We can keep our present prosperity, and increase it, only if free enterprise and free Government work together to that end.

We cannot afford to float ceaselessly on a post-war boom until it collapses. It is not enough merely to prepare to weather a recession if it comes. Instead, government and business must work together constantly to achieve more and more jobs and more and more production—which mean more and more prosperity for all the people.

The business cycle is man-made; and men of good-will, working together, can smooth it out.

So far as business is concerned, it should plan for steady, vigorous expansion—seeking always to increase its output, lower its prices, and avoid the vices of monopoly and restrictions. So long as business does this, it will be contributing to continued prosperity and it will have the help and encouragement of the Government. . . .

One of the most important factors in maintaining prosperity is the Government's fiscal policy. At this time it is essential not only that the Federal budget be balanced but also that there be a substantial surplus to reduce inflationary pressures and to permit a sizeable reduction in the national debt, which now stands as $252 billion.

I recommend, therefore, that the Congress enact new tax legislation to bring in an additional $4 billion of Government revenue. This should come principally from additional corporate taxes. A portion should come from revised estate and gift taxes. Consideration should be given to raising personal income tax rates in the middle and upper brackets.

If we want to keep our economy running to high gear we must be sure that every group has the incentive to make its full contribution to the national welfare. At present the working men and women of the nation are unfairly discriminated against by a statute that abridges their rights, curtails their constructive efforts and hampers our system of free collective bargaining. That statute is the Labor-Management Relations Act of 1947, sometimes called the Taft-Hartley Act.

That act should be repealed.

The Wagner Act should be reenacted. . . .

The health of our economy and its maintenance at high levels further require that the minimum wage fixed by law should be raised to at least 75 cents an hour.

If our free enterprise economy is to be strong and healthy we must reinvigorate the forces of competition. We must assure small business the freedom and opportunity to grow and prosper. To this purpose, we should strengthen our anti-trust laws by closing those loopholes that permit monopolistic mergers and consolidations.

Our national farm program should be improved—not only in the interest of the farmers but for the lasting prosperity of the whole nation. Our goals should be abundant farm production and parity income for agriculture. Standards of living on the farm should be just as good as anywhere else.

Farm price supports are an essential part of our program to achieve these ends. Price supports should be used to prevent farm price declines which are out of line with general price levels, to facilitate adjustments in production to consumer demands, and to promote good land use. Our price support legislation must be adapted to these objectives. The authority of the Commodity Credit Corporation to provide adequate storage space for crops should be restored.

Our program for farm prosperity should also seek to expand the domestic market for agricultural products, particularly among low income groups, and to increase and stabilize foreign markets.

We should give special attention to extending modern conveniences and services to our farms. Rural electrification should be pushed forward. And in considering legislation relating to housing, education, health and social security, special attention should be given to rural problems.

Our growing population and the expansion of our economy depends upon the wise management of our land, water, forest and mineral wealth. In our present dynamic economy the task of conservation is not to lock up our resources, but to develop and improve them. Failure, today, to make the investments which are necessary to support our progress in the future would be false economy.

We must push forward the development of our rivers for power, irrigation, navigation and flood control. We should apply the lessons of our Tennessee Valley experience to our other great river basins.

I again recommend action be taken by the Congress to approve the St. Lawrence Seaway and Power Project. This is about the fifth time I've recommended it.

We must adopt a program for the planned use of the petroleum reserves under the sea, which are—and must remain—vested in the Federal Government. We must extend our programs of soil conservation. We must place our forests on a sustained yield basis and encourage the development of new sources of vital minerals.

In all this we must make sure that the benefits of these public undertakings are directly available to the people. Public power should be carried to consuming areas by public transmission lines where necessary to provide electricity at the lowest possible rates. Irrigation waters should serve family farms and not land speculators.

The Government has still other opportunities—to help raise the standard of living of our citizens. These opportunities lie in the fields of social security, health, education, housing and civil rights.

The present coverage of the social security laws is altogether inadequate, and benefit payments are too low. One-third of our workers are not covered. Those who receive old age and survivors insurance benefits receive an average payment of only $25 a month. Many others who cannot work because they are physically disabled are left to the mercy of charity.

We should expand our social security program, both as to the size of the benefits and extent of coverage, against the economic hazards due to unemployment, old age, sickness, and disability.

We must spare no effort to raise the general level of health in this country. In a nation as rich as ours it is a shocking fact that tens of millions lack adequate medical care. We are short of doctors, hospitals and nurses. We must remedy these shortages. Moreover, we need—and we must have without further delay—a system of pre-paid medical insurance which will enable every American to afford good medical care.

It is equally shocking that millions of our children are not receiving a good education. Millions of them are in overcrowded, obsolete buildings. We are short of teachers, because teachers' salaries are too low to attract new teachers, or to hold the ones we have. All these school problems will become much more acute as a result of the tremendous increase in the enrollment in our elementary schools in the next few years.

I cannot repeat too strongly my desire for prompt Federal financial aid to the states to help them operate and maintain their school systems.

The Governmental agency which now administers the programs of health, education and social security should be given full departmental status.

The housing shortage continues to be acute. As an immediate step, the Congress should enact the provisions of low-rent public housing, slum clearance, farm housing and housing research which I have repeatedly recommended. The number of low-rent public housing units provided for in the legislation should be increased to 1,000,000 units in the next seven years. Even this number of units will not begin to meet our need for new housing.

Most of the houses we need will have to be built by private enterprise, without public subsidy. By producing too few rental units and too large a proportion of high-priced houses, the building industry is rapidly pricing itself out of the market. Building costs must be lowered.

The Government is now engaged in a campaign to induce all segments of the building industry to concentrate on the production of lower priced housing. Additional legislation to encourage such housing will be submitted.

The authority which I have requested to allocate materials in short supply and to impose price ceilings on such materials, could be used, if found necessary, to channel more materials into homes large enough for family life at prices which wage earners can afford.

The driving force behind our progress is our faith in our democratic institutions. That faith is embodied in the promise of equal rights and equal opportunities which the founders of our republic proclaimed to their countrymen and to the whole world.

The fulfillment of this promise is among the highest puposes of Government . . .

INAUGURAL ADDRESS
January 20, 1949

In one of the greatest political upsets in American history, Truman defeated Governor Thomas E. Dewey of New York for the Presidency. This address reflected Truman's concept of a "Fair Deal" for the whole world.

Mr. Vice President, Mr. Chief Justice, and fellow citizens, I accept with humility the honor which the American people have conferred upon me. I accept it with a deep resolve to do all that I can for the welfare of this Nation and for the peace of the world.

In performing the duties of my office, I need the help and prayers of every one of you. I ask for your encouragement and your support. The tasks we face are difficult, and we can accomplish them only if we work together.

Each period of our national history has had its special challenges. Those that confront us now are as momentous as any in the past. Today marks the beginning not only of a new administration, but of a period that will be eventful, perhaps decisive, for us and for the world.

It may be our lot to experience, and in large measure to bring about, a major turning point in the long history of the human race. The first half of this century has been marked by unprecedented and brutal attacks on the rights of man, and by the two most frightful wars in history. The supreme need of our time is for men to learn to live together in peace and harmony.

The peoples of the earth face the future with grave uncertainty, composed almost equally of great hopes and great fears. In this time of doubt, they look to the United States as never before for good will, strength, and wise leadership.

It is fitting, therefore, that we take this occasion to proclaim to the world the essential principles of the faith by which we live, and to declare our aims to all peoples.

The American people stand firm in the faith which has inspired this Nation from the beginning. We believe that all men have a right to equal justice under law and equal opportunity to share in the common good. We believe that all men have the right to freedom of thought and expression. We believe that all men are created equal because they are created in the image of God.

From this faith we will not be moved.

The American people desire, and are determined to work for, a world in which all nations and all peoples are free to govern themselves as they see fit and to achieve a decent and satisfying life. Above all else, our people desire, and are determined to work for, peace on earth—a just and lasting peace—based on genuine agreement freely arrived at by equals.

In the pursuit of these aims, the United States and other like-minded nations find themselves directly opposed by a regime with contrary aims and a totally different concept of life.

That regime adheres to a false philosophy which purports to offer freedom, security, and greater opportunity to mankind. Misled by this philosophy, many peoples have sacrificed their liberties only to learn to their sorrow that deceit and mockery, poverty and tyranny, are their reward.

That false philosophy is communism.

Communism is based on the belief that man is so weak and inadequate that he is unable to govern himself, and therefore requires the rule of strong masters.

Democracy is based on the conviction that man has the moral and intellectual capacity, as well as the inalienable right, to govern himself with reason and justice.

Communism subjects the individual to arrest without lawful cause, punishment without trial, and forced labor as the chattel of the state. It decrees what information he shall receive, what art he shall produce, what leaders he shall follow, and what thoughts he shall think.

Democracy maintains that government is established for the benefit of the individual, and is charged with the responsibility of protecting the rights of the individual and his freedom in the exercise of his abilities.

Communism maintains that social wrongs can be corrected only by violence.

Democracy has proved that social justice can be achieved through peaceful change.

Communism holds that the world is so deeply divided into opposing classes that war is inevitable.

Democracy holds that free nations can settle differences justly and maintain lasting peace.

These differences between communism and democracy do not concern the United States alone. People everywhere are coming to realize that what is involved is material well-being, human dignity, and the right to believe in and worship God.

I state these differences, not to draw issues of belief as such, but because the actions resulting from the Communist philosophy are a threat to the efforts of free nations to bring about world recovery and lasting peace.

Since the end of hostilities, the United States has invested its substance and its energy in a great constructive effort to restore peace, stability, and freedom in the world.

We have sought no territory and we have imposed our will on none. We have asked for no privileges we would not extend to others.

We have constantly and vigorously supported the United Nations and related agencies as a means of applying democratic principles to international relations. We have consistently advocated and relied upon peaceful settlement of disputes among nations.

We have made every effort to secure agreement on effective international control of our most powerful weapon, and we have worked steadily for the limitation and control of all armaments.

We have encouraged, by precept and example, the expansion of world trade on a sound and fair basis.

Almost a year ago, in company with 16 free nations of Europe, we launched the greatest cooperative economic program in history. The purpose of that unprecedented effort is to invigorate and strengthen democracy in Europe, so that the free people of that continent can resume their rightful place in the forefront of civilization and can contribute once more to the security and welfare of the world.

Our efforts have brought new hope to all mankind. We have beaten back despair and defeatism. We have saved a number of countries from losing their liberty. Hundreds of millions of people all over the world now agree with us, that we need not have war—that we can have peace.

The initiative is ours.

We are moving on with other nations to build an even stronger structure of international order and justice. We shall have as our partners countries which, no longer solely concerned with the problems of national survival, are now working to improve the standards of living of all their people. We are ready to undertake new projects to strengthen the free world.

In the coming years, our program for peace and freedom will emphasize four major courses of action.

First. We will continue to give unfaltering support to the United Nations and related agencies, and we will continue to search for ways to strengthen their authority and increase their effectiveness. We believe that the United Nations will be strengthened by the new nations which are being formed in lands now advancing toward self-government under democratic principles.

Second. We will continue our programs for world economic recovery.

This means, first of all, that we must keep our full weight behind the European recovery program. We are confident of the success of this major venture in world recovery. We believe that our partners in this effort will achieve the status of self-supporting nations once again.

In addition, we must carry out our plans for reducing the barriers to world trade and increasing its volume. Economic recovery and peace itself depend on increased world trade.

Third. We will strengthen freedom-loving nations against the dangers of aggression.

We are now working out with a number of countries a joint agreement designed to strengthen the security of the North Atlantic area. Such an agreement would take the form of a collective defense arrangement within the terms of the United Nations Charter.

We have already established such a defense pact for the Western Hemisphere by the treaty of Rio de Janeiro.

The primary purpose of these agreements is to provide unmistakable proof of the joint determination of the free countries to resist armed attack from any quarter. Each country participating in these arrangements must contribute all it can to the common defense.

If we can make it sufficiently clear, in advance, that any armed attack affecting our national security would be met with overwhelming force, the armed attack might never occur.

I hope soon to send to the Senate a treaty respecting the North Atlantic security plan.

In addition, we will provide military advice and equipment to free nations which will cooperate with us in the maintenance of peace and security.

Fourth. We must embark on a bold new program for making the benefits our our scientific advances and industrial progress available for the improvement and growth of underdeveloped areas.

More than half the people of the world are living in conditions approaching misery. Their food is inadequate. They are victims of disease. Their economic life is primitive and stagnant. Their poverty is a handicap and a threat both to them and to more prosperous areas.

For the first time in history humanity possesses the knowledge and the skill to relieve the suffering of these people.

The United States is preeminent among nations in the development of industrial and scientific techniques. The material resources which we can afford to use for the assistance of other peoples are limited. But our imponderable resources in technical knowledge are constantly growing and are inexhaustible.

I believe that we should make available to peace-loving peoples the benefits of our store of technical knowledge in order to help them realize their aspirations for a better life. And, in cooperation with other nations, we should foster capital investment in areas needing development.

Our aim should be to help the free peoples of the world, through their own efforts, to produce more food, more clothing, more materials for housing, and more mechanical power to lighten their burdens.

We invite other countries to pool their technological resources in this undertaking. Their contributions will be warmly welcomed. This should be a cooperative enterprise in which all nations work together through the United Nations and its specialized agencies wherever practicable. It must be a world-wide effort for the achievement of peace, plenty, and freedom.

With the cooperation of business, private capital, agriculture, and labor in this country, this program can greatly increase the industrial activity in other nations and can raise substantially their standards of living.

Such new economic developments must be devised and controlled to benefit the peoples of the areas in which they are established. Guaranties to the investor must be balanced by guaranties in the interest of the people whose resources and whose labor go into these developments.

The old imperialism—exploitation for foreign profit—has no place in our plans. What we envisage is a program of deveopment based on the concepts of democratic fair dealing.

All countries, including our own, will greatly benefit from a constructive program for the better use of the world's human and natural resources. Experience shows that our commerce with other countries expands as they progress industrially and economically.

Greater production is the key to prosperity and peace. And the key to greater production is a wider and more vigorous application of modern scientific and technical knowledge.

Only by helping the least fortunate of its members to help themselves can the human family achieve the decent, satisfying life that is the right of all people.

Democracy alone can supply the vitalizing force to stir the peoples of the world into triumphant action, not only against their human oppressors, but also against their ancient enemies—hunger, misery, and despair.

On the basis of these four major courses of action we hope to help create the conditions that will lead eventually to personal freedom and happiness for all mankind.

If we are to be successful in carrying out these policies, it is clear that we must have continued prosperity in this country and we must keep ourselves strong.

Slowly but surely we are weaving a world fabric of international security and growing prosperity.

We are aided by all who wish to live in freedom from fear—even by those who live today in fear under their own governments.

We are aided by all who want relief from the lies of propaganda—who desire truth and sincerity.

We are aided by all who desire self-government and a voice in deciding their own affairs.

We are aided by all who long for economic security—for the security and abundance that men in free societies can enjoy.

We are aided by all who desire freedom of speech, freedom of religion, and freedom to live their own lives for useful ends . . .

ON POINT FOUR
June 24, 1949

Truman, in his inaugural address, had outlined the Point Four program for economic assistance to underdeveloped countries throughout the world. In this message he urged Congress to enact the necessary legislation.

In order to enable the United States, in cooperation with other countries, to assist the peoples of economically underdeveloped areas to raise their standards of living, I recommend the enactment of legislation to authorize an expanded program of technical assistance for such areas, and an experimental program for encouraging the outflow of private investement beneficial to their economic development. These measures are the essential first steps in an undertaking which will call upon private enterprise and voluntary organizations in the United States, as well as the government, to take part in a constantly growing effort to improve economic conditions in the less developed regions of the world.

The grinding poverty and the lack of economic opportunity for many millions of people in the economically underdeveloped parts of Africa, the Near and Far East, and certain regions of Central and South America, constitute one of the greatest challenges of the world today. In spite of their age-old economic and social handicaps, the peoples in these areas have, in recent decades, been stirred and awakened. The spread of industrial civilization, the growing understanding of modern concepts of government, and the impact of two World Wars have changed their lives and their outlook. They are eager to play a greater part in the community of nations.

All these areas have a common problem. They must create a firm economic base for the democratic aspirations of their citizens. Without such an economic base, they will be unable to meet the expectations which the modern world has aroused in their peoples. If they are frustrated and disappointed, they may turn to false doctrines which hold that the way of progress lies through tyranny.

For the United States the great awakening of these peoples holds tremendous promise. It is not only a promise that new and stronger nations will be associated with us in the cause of human freedom, it is also a promise of new economic strength and growth for ourselves.

With many of the economically underdeveloped areas of the world, we have long had ties of trade and commerce. In many instances today we greatly need the products of their labor and their resources. If the productivity and the purchasing power of these countries are expanded, our own industry and agriculture will benefit. Our experience shows that the volume of our foreign trade is far greater with highly developed countries than it is with countries having a low standard of living and inadequate industry. To increase the output and the national income of the less developed regions is to increase our own economic stability.

In addition, the development of these areas is of utmost importance to our efforts to restore the economies of the free European nations. As the economies of the underdeveloped areas expand, they will provide needed products for Europe and will offer a better market for European goods. Such expansion is an essential part of the growing system of world trade which is necessary for European recovery.

Furthermore, the development of these areas will strengthen the United Nations and the fabric of world peace. The preamble to the Charter of the United Nations states that the economic and social advancement of all people is an essential bulwark of peace. Under article 56 of the Charter, we have promised to take separate action and to act jointly with other nations "to promote higher standards of living, full employment, and conditions of economic and social progress and development."

For these various reasons, assistance in the development of the economically underdeveloped areas has become one of the major elements of our foreign policy. In my inaugural address, I outlined a program to help the peoples of these areas to attain greater production as a way to prosperity and peace.

The major effort in such a program must be local in character; it must be made by the people of the underdeveloped areas themselves. It is essential, however, to the success of their effort that there be help from abroad. In some cases, the peoples of these areas will be unable to begin their part of this great enterprise without initial aid from other countries.

The aid that is needed falls roughly into two categories. The first is the technical, scientific, and managerial knowledge necessary to economic development. This category includes not only medial and educational knowledge, and assistance and advice in such basic fields as sanitation, communications, road building, and governmental services, but also, and perhaps most important, assistance in the survey of resources and in planning for long-range economic development.

The second category is production goods—machinery and equipment—and financial assistance in the creation of productive enterprises. The underdeveloped areas need capital for port and harbor development, roads and communications, irrigation and drainage projects, as well as for public utilities and the whole range of extractive, processing, and manufacturing industries. Much of the capital required can be provided by these areas themselves, in spite of their low standards of living. But much must come from abroad.

The two categories of aid are closely related. Technical assistance is necessary to lay the ground-work for productive investment. Investment, in turn, brings with it technical assistance. In general, however, technical surveys of resources and of the possibilities of economic development must precede substantial capital investment. Furthermore, in many of the areas concerned, technical assistance in improving sanitation, communications, or education is required to create conditions in which capital investment can be fruitful.

This country, in recent years, has conducted relatively modest programs of technical cooperation with other countries. In the field of education, channels of exchange and communication have been opened between our citizens and those of other countries. To some extent, the expert assistance of a number of Federal agencies, such as the Public Health Service and the Department of Agriculture, has been made available to other countries. We have also participated in the activities of the United Nations, its specialized agencies, and other international organizations to disseminate useful techniques among nations.

Through these various activities, we have gained considerable experience in rendering technical assistance to other countries. What is needed now is to expand and integrate these activities and to concentrate them particularly on the economic development of underdeveloped areas.

Much of the aid that is needed can be provided most effectively through the United Nations. Shortly after my inaugural address, this government asked the Economic and Social Council of the United Nations to consider what the United Nations and the specialized international agencies could do in this program.

The Secretary-General of the United Nations thereupon asked the United Nations Secretariat and the Secretariats of the specialized international agencies to draw up cooperative plans for technical assistance to underdeveloped areas. As a result, a survey was made of technical projects suitable for these agencies in such fields as industry, labor, agrculture, scientific research with respect to natural resources, and fiscal management. The total cost of the program submitted as a result of this survey was estimated to be about 35 million dollars for the first year. It is expected that the United Nations and the specialized international agencies will shortly adopt programs for carrying out projects of the type included in this survey.

In addition to our participation in this work of the United Nations, much of the technical assistance required can be provided directly by the United States to countries needing it. A careful examination of the existing information concerning the underdeveloped countries shows particular need for technicians and experts with United States training in plant and animal diseases, malaria and typhus control, water supply and sewer systems, metallurgy and mining, and nearly all phases of industry.

It has already been shown that experts in these fields can bring about tremendous improvements. For example, the health of the people of many foreign communities has been greatly improved by the work of United States sanitary engineers in setting up modern water supply systems. The food supply of many areas has been increased as the result of the advice of United States agricultural experts in the control of animal diseases and the improvement of crops. These are only examples of the wide range of benefits resulting from the careful application of modern techniques to local problems. The benefits which a comprehensive program of expert assistance will make possible can only be revealed by studies and surveys undertaken as a part of the program itself.

To inaugurate the program, I recommend a first year appropriation of not to exceed 45 million dollars. This includes 10 million dollars already requested in the 1950 Budget for activities of this character. The sum recommended will cover both our participation in the programs of the international agencies and the assistance to be provided directly by the United States . . .

STATE OF THE UNION MESSAGE
January 4, 1950

In a rather general statement, Truman, again, stressed the connection between American economic prosperity and foreign policy.

Mr. President, Mr. Speaker, Members of the Congress:

A year ago I reported to this Congress that the state of the Union was good. I am happy to be able to report to you today that the state of the Union continues to be good. Our Republic continues to increase in the enjoyment of freedom within its borders, and to offer strength and encouragement to all those who love freedom throughout the world.

During the past year we have made notable progress in strengthening the foundations of peace and freedom, abroad and at home.

We have taken important steps in securing the North Atlantic community against aggression. We have continued our successful support of European recovery. We have returned to our established policy of expanding international trade through reciprocal agreement. We have strengthened our support of the United Nations.

While great problems still confront us, the greater danger has receded— the possibility which faced us 3 years ago that most of Europe and the Mediterranean area might collapse under totalitarian pressure. Today, the free peoples of the world have new vigor and new hope for the cause of peace.

In our domestic affairs, we have made notable advances toward broader opportunity and a better life for all our citizens.

We have met and reversed the first significant downturn in economic activity since the war. In accomplishing this, Government programs for maintaining employment and purchasing power have been of tremendous benefit. As the result of these programs, and the wisdom and good judgment of our businessmen and workers, major readjustments have been made without widespread suffering.

During the past year, we have also made a good start in providing housing for low-income groups; we have raised minimum wages; we have gone forward with the development of our natural resources; we have given a greater assurance of stability to the farmer; and we have improved the organization and efficiency of our Government.

Today, by the grace of God, we stand a free and prosperous nation with greater possibilities for the future than any people ever had before in the history of the world.

We are now, in this year of 1950, nearing the midpoint of the 20th century.

The first half of this century will be known as the most turbulent and eventful period in recorded history. The swift pace of events promises to make the next 50 years decisive in the history of man on this planet.

The scientific and industrial revolution which began two centuries ago has, in the last 50 years, caught up the peoples of the globe in a common destiny. Two world-shattering wars have proved that no corner of the earth can be isolated from the affairs of mankind.

The human race has reached a turning point. Man has opened the secrets of nature and mastered new powers. If he uses them wisely, he can reach new heights of civilization. If he uses them foolishly, they may destroy him.

Man must create the moral and legal framework for the world which will insure that his new powers are used for good and not for evil. In shaping the outcome, the people of the United States will play a leading role.

Among all the great changes that have occurred in the last 50 years, none is more important that the change in the position of the United States in world affairs. Fifty years ago we were a country devoted largely to our own internal affairs. Our industry was growing, and we had new interests in the Far East and in the Caribbean, but we were primarily concerned with the development of vast areas of our own continental territory. . . .

Under the principles of the United Nations Charter we must continue to share in the common defense of free nations against aggression. At the last session this Congress laid the basis for this joint effort. We now must put into effect the common defense plans that are being worked out.

We shall continue our efforts for world economic recovery, because world prosperity is the only sure foundation of a permanent peace.

As an immediate means to this end we must continue our support of the European recovery program. This program has achieved great success in the first 2 years of its operation, but it has not yet been completed. If we were to stop this program now, or cripple it, just because it is succeeding, we should be doing exactly what the enemies of democracy want us to do. We should be just as foolish as a man who, for reasons of false economy, failed to put a roof on his house after building the foundation and the walls.

World prosperity also requires that we do all we can to expand world trade. As a major step in this direction we should promptly join the International Trade Organization. The purpose of this organization, which the United States has been foremost in creating, is to establish a code of fair practice, and an international authority for adjusting differences in international commercial relations. It is an effort to prevent the kind of anarchy and irresponsibility in world trade which did so much to bring about the world depression of the 1930's.

An expanding world economy requires the improvement of living standards and the development of resources in areas where human poverty and misery now prevail. Without such improvement the recovery of Europe and the future of our own economy will not be secure. I urge that the Congress adopt the legislation now before it to provide for increasing the flow of technical assistance and capital investment in underdeveloped regions.

It is more essential now than ever, if the ideals of freedom and representative government are to prevail in these areas, and particularly in the Far East, that their peoples experience, in their own lives, the benefits of scientific and economic advances. This program will require the movement of large amounts of capital from the industrial nations, and particularly from the United States, to productive uses in the underdeveloped areas of the world. Recent world events make prompt action imperative.

This program is in the interest of all peoples—and has nothing in common with either with the old imperialism of the last century or the new imperialism of the Communists.

Our aim for a peaceful, democratic world of free peoples will be achieved in the long run, not by force of arms, but by an appeal to the minds and hearts of men. If the peace policy of the democratic nations is to be successful, they must demonstrate that the benefits of their way of life can be increased and extended to all nations and all races.

In the world today we are confronted with the danger that the rising demand of people everywhere for freedom and a better life may be corrupted and betrayed by the false promises of communism. In its ruthless struggle for power, communism seizes upon our imperfections, and takes advantage of the delays and setbacks which the democratic nations experience in their efforts to secure a better life for their citizens. This challenge to us is more than a military challenge. It is a challenge to the honesty of our profession of the democratic faith; it is a challenge to the efficiency and stability of our economic system; it is a challenge to the willingness to work with other peoples for world peace and for world prosperity.

For my part I welcome that challenge. I believe that our country, at this crucial point in world history, will meet that challenge successfully. I believe that, in cooperation with the other free nations of the world, we shall extend the full benefits of the democratic way of life to millions who do not now enjoy them, and preserve mankind from dictatorship and tyranny.

I believe that we shall succeed in our struggle for this peace, because I have seen the success we have had in our own country in following the principles of freedom. Over the last 50 years, the ideals of liberty and equal opportunity to which this Nation is dedicated have been increasingly realized in the lives of our people.

The ideal of equal opportunity no longer means simply the opportunity which a man has to advance beyond his fellows. Some of our citizens do achieve greater success than others as a reward for individual merit and effort, and this is as it should be. At the same time our country must be more than a land of opportunity for a select few. It must be a land of opportunity for all of us. In such a land we can grow and prosper together.

The simple truth that we can all go forward together is often questioned by selfish or shortsighted persons. It is strange that this is so, for this proposition is so clearly demonstrated by our national history. During the last 50 years, for example, our Nation has grown enormously in material well-being. This growth has come about, not by concentrating the benefits of our progress in the hands of a few, but by increasing the wealth of the great body of our Nation and our citizens.

In the last 50 years the income of the average family has increased so greatly that its buying power has doubled. The average hours of work have declined from 60 to 40 a week, the whole hourly production of the average worker has tripled. Average wages, allowing for price changes, have increased from about 45 cents an hour to $1.40 an hour.

We have accomplished what to earlier ages of mankind would have been a miracle—we work shorter hours, we produce more, and we live better.

Increasing freedom from poverty and drudgery has given a fuller meaning to American life. our people are better educated; we have more opportunities for travel and recreation and enjoyment of the arts. We enjoy more personal liberty in the United States today than ever before.

If we can continue in the spirit of cooperative adventure which has marked the recent years of our progress, we can expect further scientific advances, further increases in our standard of living, and a still wider enjoyment of democratic freedom.

No one, of course, can foretell the future exactly. However, if we assume that we shall grow as fast in the future as we have grown in the past, we can get a good idea of how much our country should grow in the next 50 years. . . .

The measures I am recommending to the Congress concerning both our foreign and our domestic policies represent a carefully considered program to meet our national needs. It is a program which necessarily requires large expenditures of funds. More than 70 percent of the Government's expenditures are required to meet the costs of past wars and to work for world peace. This is the dominant factor in our fiscal policy. At the same time, the Government must make substantial expenditures which are necessary to the growth and expansion of the domestic economy.

At present, largely because of the ill-considered tax reduction of the 80th Congress, the Government is not receiving enough revenue to meet its necessary expenditures.

To meet this situation, I am proposing that Federal expenditures be held to the lowest levels consistent with our international requirements and the essential needs of economic growth, and the well-being of our people. I think I had better read that over; you interrupted me in the middle.

To meet this situation, I am proposing that Federal expenditures be held to the lowest levels consistent with our international requirements and the essential needs of economic growth, and the well-being of our people. Don't forget that last phrase. At the same time, we must guard against the folly of attempting budget slashes which would impair our prospects for peace or cripple the programs essential to our national strength.

The budget recommendations I shall shortly transmit to the Congress show that we can expect a substantial improvement in our fiscal position over the next few years, as the cost of some of our extraordinary postwar programs declines, and as the Government revenue rises as a result of growth in employment and national income. To further improve our fiscal outlook, we should make some changes in our tax system which will reduce present inequities, stimulate business activity, and yield a moderate amount of additional revenue. I expect to transmit specific recommendations to the Congress on this subject at a very early date.

The fiscal policy I am recommending is the quickest and safest way of achieving a balanced budget.

As we move forward into the second half of the 20th century, we must always bear in mind the central purpose of our national life. We do not seek material prosperity for ourselves because we love luxury; we do not aid other nations because we wish to increase our power. We have not devised programs for the security and well-being of our people becuase we are afraid or unwilling to take risks. This is not the meaning of our past history or our present course.

We work for a better life for all, so that all men may put to good use the great gifts with which they have been endowed by their Creator. We seek to establish those material conditions of life in which, without exception, men may live in dignity, perform useful work, serve their communities, and worship God as they see fit . . .

ON HYDROGEN BOMB PROGRAM
January 31, 1950

Truman announced the inauguration of an all-out effort to develop a hydrogen bomb substantially more powerful than existing atomic weapons. This program achieved its initial objective in November, 1952, when the first hydrogen bomb was detonated.

It is part of my responsibility as Commander-in-Chief of the armed forces to see to it that our country is able to defend itself against any possible aggressor. Accordingly, I have directed the Atomic Energy Commission to continue its work on all forms of atomic weapons, including the so-called hydrogen or super-bomb. Like all other work in the field of atomic weapons, it is being and will be carried forward on a basis consistent with the over-all objectives of our program for peace and security.

This we shall continue to do until a satisfactory plan for international control of atomic energy is achieved. We shall also continue to examine all those factors that affect our program for peace and this country's security.

The activities necessary to carry out our program of technical aid will be diverse in character and will have to be performed by a number of different government agencies and private instrumentalities. It will be necessary to utilize not only the resources of international agencies and the United States Government, but also the facilities and the experience of the private business and non-profit organizations that have long been active in this work. . . .

In the economically underdeveloped areas of the world today there are new creative energies. We look forward to the time when these countries will be stronger and more independent than they are now, and yet more closely bound to us and to other nations by ties of friendship and commerce, and by kindred ideals. On the other hand, unless we aid the newly awakened spirit in these peoples to find the course of fruitful development, they may fall under the control of those whose philosophy is hostile to human freedom, thereby prolonging the unsettled state of the world and postponing the achievement of permanent peace.

Before the peoples of these areas we hold out the promise of a better future through the democratic way of life. It is vital that we move quickly to bring the meaning of that promise home to them in their daily lives.

HARRY S TRUMAN

ON THE OUTBREAK OF THE KOREAN WAR
June 27, 1950

On June 25, 1950, the North Koreans launched a full scale attack on the South. Two days later, the U.N. Security Council called on all members to repel the attack and restore peace.

In Korea the Government forces, which were armed to prevent border raids and to preserve internal security, were attacked by invading forces from North Korea. The Security Council of the United Nations called upon the invading troops to cease hostilities and to withdraw to the 38th parallel. This they have not done, but on the contrary have pressed the attack. The Security Council called upon all members of the United Nations to render every assistance to the United Nations in the execution of this resolution. In these circumstances I have ordered United States air and sea forces to give the Korean Government troops cover and support.

The attack upon Korea makes it plain beyond all doubt that Communism has passed beyond the use of subversion to conquer independent nations and will now use armed invasion and war. It has defied the orders of the Security Council of the United Nations issued to preserve international peace and security. In these circumstances the occupation of Formosa by Communist forces would be a direct threat to the security of the Pacific area and to the United States forces performing their lawful and necessary functions in that area. Accordingly I have ordered the Seventh Fleet to prevent any attack on Formosa. As a corollary of this action I am calling upon the Chinese Government on Formosa to cease all air and sea operations against the mainland. The Seventh Fleet will see that this is done. The determination of the future status of Formosa must await the restoration of security in the Pacific, a peace settlement with Japan, or consideration by the United Nations.

I have also directed that United States Forces in the Philippines be strengthened and that military assistance to the Philippine Government be accelerated.

I have similarly directed acceleration in the furnishing of military assistance to the forces of France and the Associated States in Indo-China and the dispatch of a military mission to provide close working relations with those forces.

I know that all members of the United Nations will consider carefully the consequences of this latest aggression in Korea in defiance of the Charter of the United Nations. A return to the rule of force in international affairs would have far reaching effects. The United States will continue to uphold the rule of law.

I have instructed Ambassador Austin, as the representative of the United States to the Security Council, to report these steps to the Council.

STATE OF THE UNION MESSAGE
January 8, 1951

In a very long annual message, Truman spoke of his determination to continue in Korea, and to strengthen his ties with the free nations of the West.

Mr. Prssident, Mr. Speaker, Members of the Congress:

This 82nd Congress faces as grave a task as any Congress in the history of our Republic. The actions you take will be watched by the whole world. These actions will measure the ability of a free people, acting through their chosen representatives and their free institutions, to meet a deadly challenge to their way of life.

We can meet this challenge foolishly or wisely. We can meet it timidly or bravely, shamefully or honorably.

I know that the 82nd Congress will meet this challenge in a way worthy of our great heritage. I know that your debates will be earnest, responsible, constructive, and to the point. I know that from these debates there will come the great decisions needed to carry us forward.

At this critical time, I am glad to say that our country is in a healthy condition. Our democratic institutions are sound and strong. We have more men and women at work than ever before. We are able to produce more than ever before—in fact, far more than any country ever produced in the history of the world.

I am confident that we can succeed in the great task that lies before us.

We will succeed, but we must all do our part. We must all act together as citizens of this great Republic.

As we meet here today, American soldiers are fighting a bitter campaign in Korea. We pay tribute to their courage, devotion, and gallantry.

Our men are fighting, alongside their United Nations allies, because they know, as we do, that the aggression in Korea is part of the attempt of the Russian Communist dictatorship to take over the world, step by step.

Our men are fighting a long way from home, but they are fighting for our lives and our liberties. They are fighting to protect our right to meet here today—our right to govern ourselves as a free nation.

The threat of world conquest by Soviet Russia endangers our liberty and endangers the kind of work in which the free spirit of man can survive. This threat is aimed at all peoples who strive to win or defend their own freedom and national independence.

Indeed, the state of our Nation is in great part the state of our friends and allies throughout the world. The gun that points at them points at us, also. The threat is a total threat and the danger is a common danger.

All free nations are exposed and all are in peril. Their only security lies in banding together. No one nation can find protection in a selfish search for a safe haven from the storm.

The free nations do not have any aggressive purpose. We want only peace in the world—peace for all countries. No threat to the security of any nation is concealed in our plans and programs.

We had hoped that the Soviet Union, with its security assured by the Charter of the United Nations, would be willing to live and let live. But I am sorry to say that has not been the case.

The imperialism of the czars has been replaced by the even more ambitious, more crafty, and more menacing imperialism of the rulers of the Soviet Union.

This new imperialism has powerful military forces. It is keeping millions of men under arms. It has a large air force and a strong submarine force. It has complete control of the men and equipment of its satellites. It has kept its subject peoples and its economy in a state of perpetual mobilization.

The present rulers of the Soviet Union have shown that they are willing to use this power to destroy the free nations and win domination over the whole world.

The Soviet imperialists have two ways of going about their destructive work. They use the method of subversion and internal revolution, and they use the method of external aggression. In preparation for either of these methods of attack, they stir up class strife and disorder. They encourage sabotage. They put out poisonous propaganda. They deliberately try to prevent economic improvement.

If their efforts are successful, they foment a revolution, as they did in Czechoslovakia and China, and as they tried, unsuccessfully, to do in Greece. If their methods of subversion are blocked, and if they think they can get away with outright warfare, they resort to external aggression. This is what they did when they loosed the armies of their puppet states against the Republic of Korea, in an evil war by proxy.

We of the free world must be ready to meet both of these methods of Soviet action. We must not neglect one or the other . . . .

Our own national security is deeply involved with that of the other free nations. While they need our support, we equally need theirs. Our national safety would be gravely prejudiced if the Soviet Union were to succeed in harnessing to its war machine the resources and the manpower of the free nations on the borders of its empire.

If Western Europe were to fall to Soviet Russia, it would double the Soviet supply of coal and triple the Soviet supply of steel. If the free countries of Asia and Africa should fall to Soviet Russia, we would lose the sources of many of our most vital raw materials, including uranium, which is the basis of our atomic power. And Soviet command of the manpower of the free nations of Europe and Asia would confront us with military forces which we could never hope to equal.

In such a situation, the Soviet Union could impose its demands on the world, without resort to conflict, simply through the preponderance of its economic and military power. The Soviet Union does not have to attack the United States to secure domination of the world. It can achieve its ends by isolating us and swallowing up all our allies. Therefore, even if we were craven enough—I do not believe we could be—but, I say, even if we were craven enough to abandon our ideals, it would be disastrous for us to withdraw from the community of free nations.

We are the most powerful single member of this community, and we have a special responsibility. We must take the leadership in meeting the challenge to freedom and in helping to protect the rights of independent nations.

This country has a practical, ralistic program of action for meeting this challenge.

First, we shall have to extend economic assistance, where it can be effective. The best way to stop subversion by the Kremlin is to strike at the roots of social injustice and economic disorder. People who have jobs, homes, and hopes for the future will defend themselves against the underground agents of the Kremlin. Our programs of economic aid have done much to turn back communism. . . .

Second, we shall need to continue our military assistance to countries which want to defend themselves.

The heart of our common defense effort is the North Atlantic community. The defense of Europe is the basis for the defense of the whole free world—ourselves included. Next to the United States, Europe is the largest workshop in the world. It is also a homeland of the great religious beliefs shared by many of our citizens—beliefs which are now threatened by the tide of atheistic communism.

Strategically, economically, and morally, the defense of Europe is a part of our own defense. That is why we have joined with the countries of Europe in the North Atlantic Treaty, pledging ourselves to work with them.

We are willing, as we have always been, to negotiate honorable settlements with the Soviet Union. But we will not engage in appeasement.

The Soviet rulers have made it clear that we must have strength as well as right on our side. If we build our strength—and we are building it—the Soviet rulers may face the facts and lay aside their plans to take over the world.

That is what we hope will happen, and that is what we are trying to bring about. That is the only realistic road to peace.

These are the main elements of the course our Nation must follow as a member of the community of free nations. These are the things we must do to preserve our security and help create a peaceful world. But they will be successful only if we increase the strength of our own country.

Here at home we have some very big jobs to do. We are building much stronger military forces—and we are building them fast. We are preparing for full wartime mobilization, if that should be necessary. And we are continuing to build a strong and growing economy, able to maintain whatever effort may be required for as long as necessary.

We are building our own Army, Navy, and Air Force to an active strength of nearly 3½ million men and women. We are stepping up the training of the reserve forces, and establishing more training facilities, so that we can rapidly increase our active forces far more on short notice.

We are going to produce all the weapons and equipment that such an armed force will need. Furthermore, we will make weapons for our allies, and weapons for our own reserve supplies. On top of this, we will build the capacity to turn out on short notice arms and supplies that may be needed for a full-scale war.

Fortunately, we have a good start on this because of our enormous plant capacity and because of the equipment on hand from the last war. For example, many combat ships are being returned to active duty from the "mothball fleet'" and many others can be put into service on very short notice. We have large reserves of arms and ammunition and thousands of workers skilled in arms production.

In many cases, however, our stocks of weapons are low. In other cases, those on hand are not the most modern. We have made remarkable technical advances. We have developed new types of jet planes and powerful new tanks. We are concentrating on producing the newest types of weapons and producing them as fast as we can.

This production drive is more selective than the one we had during World War II, but it is just as urgent and intense. It is a big program and it is a costly one.

Let me give you two concrete examples.

Our present program calls for expanding the aircraft industry so that it will have the capacity to produce 50,000 modern military planes a year. We are preparing the capacity to produce 35,000 tanks a year. We are not now ordering that many planes or that many tanks, and we hope that we never have to, but we mean to be able to turn them out if we need them.

The planes we are producing now are much bigger, much better, and much more expensive than the planes we had during the last war.

We used to think that the B-17 was a hugh plane, and the blockbuster it carried a hugh load. But the B-36 can carry five of these blockbusters in its belly, and it can carry them five times as far. Of course, the B-36 is much more complicated to build than the B-17, and far more expensive. One B-17 costs $275,000, while now one B-36 costs $3½ million.

I ask you to remember that what we are doing is to provide the best and most modern military equipment in the world for our fighting forces.

This kind of defense production program has two parts.

The first part is to get our defense production going as fast as possible.

We have to convert plants and channel materials to defense production. This means heavy cuts in civilian uses of copper, aluminum, rubber, and other essential materials. It means shortages in various consumer goods.

The second part is to increase our capacity to produce and to keep our economy strong for the long pull. We do not know how long Communist aggression will threaten the world.

Only by increasing our output can we carry the burden of preparedness for an indefinite period in the future. This means that we will have to build more power plants and more steel mills, grow more cotton, mine more copper, and expand our capacity in many other ways.

The Congress will need to consider legislation, at this session, affecting all the aspects of our mobilization job. The main subjects on which legislation will be needed are:

First, appropriations for our military buildup.

Second, extension and revision of the Selective Service Act.

Third, military and economic aid to help build up the strength of the free world.

Fourth, revision and extension of the authority to expand production and to stabilize prices, wages, and rents.

Fifth, improvement of our agricultural laws to help obtain the kinds of farm products we need for the defense effort.

Sixth, improvement of our labor laws to help provide stable labor-management relations and to make sure that we have steady production in this emergency.

Seventh, housing and training of defense workers and the full use of all our manpower resources.

Eighth, means for increasing the supply of doctors, nurses, and other trained medical personnel critically needed for the defense effort.

Ninth, aid to the States to meet the most urgent needs of our elementary and secondary schools. Some of our plans will have to be deferred for the time being. But we should do all we can to make sure our children are being trained as good and useful citizens in the critical times ahead.

Tenth, a major increase in taxes to meet the cost of the defense effort.

The Economic Report and the Budget Message will discuss these subjects further. In addition, I shall send to the Congress special messages containing detailed recommendations on legislation needed at this session.

In the months ahead the Government must give priority to activities that are urgent—like military procurement and atomic energy and power development. It must practice rigid economy in its non-defense activities. Many of the things we would normally do must be curtailed or postponed.

But in a long-term defense effort like this one, we cannot neglect the measures needed to maintain a strong economy and a healthy democratic society . . .

THE RECALL OF GENERAL MacARTHUR
April 16, 1951

MacArthur proposed the use of air and naval forces to extend the Korean war to Chinese territory. Truman believed in a limited war and ordered MacArthur to carry out this military program.

I want to talk plainly to you tonight about what we are doing in Korea and about our policy in the Far East.

In the simplest terms, what we are doing in Korea is this: We are trying to prevent a third world war.

I think most people in this country recognized that fact last June. And they warmly supported the decision of the Government to help the Republic of Korea against the Communist aggressors. Now, many persons, even some who applauded our decision to defend Korea, have forgotten the basic reason for our action.

It is right for us to be in Korea. It was right last June. It is right today.

I want to remind you why this is true.

The Communists in the Kremlin are engaged in a monstrous conspiracy to stamp out freedom all over the world. If they were to succeed, the United States would be numbered among their principal victims. It must be clear to everyone that the United States cannot—and will not—sit idly by and await foreign conquest. The only question is: When is the best time to meet the threat and how?

The best time to meet the threat is in the beginning. It is easier to put out a fire in the beginning when it is small than after it has become a roaring blaze.

And the best way to meet the threat of aggression is for the peace-loving nations to act together. If they don't act together, they are likely to be picked off, one by one. . . .

This is the basic reason why we joined in creating the United Nations. And since the end of World War II we have been putting that lesson into practice—we have been working with other free nations to check the aggressive designs of the Soviet Union before they can result in a third world war.

That is what we did in Greece, when that nation was threatened by the aggression of international communism.

The attack against Greece could have led to general war. But this country came to the aid of Greece. The United Nations supported Greek resistance. With our help, the determination and efforts of the Greek people defeated the attack on the spot.

Another big Communist threat to peace was the Berlin blockade. That too could have led to war. But again it was settled because free men would not back down in an emergency. . . .

The question we have had to face is whether the Communist plan of conquest can be stopped without general war. Our Government and other countries associated with us in the United Nations believe that the best chance of stopping it without general war is to meet the attack in Korea and defeat it there.

That is what we have been doing. It is a difficult and bitter task.

But so far it has been successful.

So far, we have prevented World War III.

So far, by fighting a limited war in Korea, we have prevented aggression from succeeding and bringing on a general war. And the ability of the whole free world to resist Communist aggression has been greatly improved.

We have taught the enemy a lesson. He has found out that aggression is not cheap or easy. Moreover, men all over the world who want to remain free have been given new courage and new hope. They know now that the champions of freedom can stand up and fight and that they will stand up and fight.

Our resolute stand in Korea is helping the forces of freedom now fighting in Indo-china and other countries in that part of the world. It has already slowed down the timetable of conquest. . . .

We do not want to see the conflict in Korea extended. We are trying to prevent a world war—not to start one. The best way to do this is to make plain that we and the other free countries will continue to resist the attack.

But you may ask: Why can't we take other steps to punish the aggressor? Why don't we bomb Manchuria and China itself? Why don't we assist Chinese Nationalist troops to land on the mainland of China?

If we were to do these things we would be running a very grave risk of starting a general war. If that were to happen, we would have brought about the exact situation we are trying to prevent.

If we were to do these things, we would become entangled in a vast conflict on the continent of Asia and our task would become immeasurably more difficult all over the world.

What would suit the ambitions of the Kremlin better than for our military forces to be committed to a full-scale war with Red China? . . .

The course we have been following is the one best calculated to avoid an all-out war. It is the course consistent with our obligations to do all we can to maintain international peace and security. Our experience in Greece and Berlin shows that it is the most effective course of action we can follow. . . .

If the Communist authorities realize that they cannot defeat us in Korea, if they realize it would be foolhardy to widen the hostilities beyond Korea, then they may recognize the folly of continuing their aggression. A peaceful settlement may then be possible. The door is always open.

Then we may achieve a settlement in Korea which will not compromise the principles and purposes of the United Nations.

I have thought long and hard about this question of extending the war in Asia. I have discussed it many times with the ablest military advisers in the country. I believe with all my heart that the course we are following is the best course.

I believe that we must try to limit war to Korea for these vital reasons: to make sure that the precious lives of our fighting men are not wasted; to see that the security of our country and the free world is not needlessly jeopardized; and to prevent a third world war.

A number of events have made it evident that General MacArthur did not agree with that policy. I have therefore considered it essential to relieve General MacArthur so that there would be no doubt or confusion as to the real purpose and aim of our policy.

It was with the deepest personal regret that I found myself compelled to take this action. General MacArthur is one of our greatest military commanders. But the cause of world peace is more important than any individual.

The change in commands in the Far East means no change whatever in the policy of the United States. We will carry on the fight in Korea with vigor and determination in an effort to bring the war to a speedy and successful conclusion.

The new commander, Lt. Gen. Matthew Ridgway, has already demonstrated that he has the great qualities of military leadership needed for this task.

We are ready, at any time, to negotiate for a restoration of peace in the area. But we will not engage in appearsement. We are only interested in real peace.

Real peace can be achieved through a settlement based on the following factors:

One: the fighting must stop.

Two: concrete steps must be taken to insure that the fighting will not break out again.

Three: there must be an end to the aggression.

A settlement founded upon these elements would open the way for the unification of Korea and the withdrawal of all foreign forces.

In the meantime, I want to be clear about our military objective. We are fighting to resist an outrageous aggression in Korea. We are trying to keep the Korean conflict from spreading to other areas. But at the same time we must conduct our military activities so as to insure the security of our forces. This is essential if they are to continue the fight until the enemy abandons its ruthless attempt to destroy the Republic of Korea.

That is our military objective—to repel attack and to restore peace . . .

STATE OF THE UNION MESSAGE
January 9, 1952

*In this short annual message, Truman assessed the accomplish-
ments of the past year, and called for political unity among all
parties despite the fact that it was a Presidential election year.*

Mr. President, Mr. Speaker, Members of the Congress:

I have the honor to report to the Congress on the state of the Union.

At the outset, I should like to speak of the necessity for putting first things
first as we work together this year for the good of our country.

The United States and the whole free world are passing through a period
of grave danger. Every action you take here in Congress, and every action
that I take as President, must be measured against the test of whether it helps
to meet that danger.

This will be a presidential election year—the year in which politics plays
a large part in our lives—a larger part than usual. That is perfectly proper.
But we have a greater responsibility to conduct our political fights in a manner that does not harm the national interest.

We can find plenty of things to differ about without destroying our free
institutions and without abandoning our bipartisan foreign policy for peace.

When everything is said and done, all of us—Republicans and Democrats
alike—all of us are Americans; and we are all going to sink or swim
together.

We are moving through a perilous time. Faced with a terrible threat of
aggression, our Nation has embarked upon a great effort to help establish
the kind of world in which peace shall be secure. Peace is our goal—not
peace at any price, but a peace based on freedom and justice. We are now in
the midst of our effort to reach that goal. On the whole, we have been doing
very well.

Last year, 1951, was a year in which we threw back aggression, added
greatly to our military strength, and improved the chances for peace and
freedom in many parts of the world.

This year, 1952, is a critical year in the defense effort of the whole free
world. If we falter we can lose all the gains we have made. If we drive ahead,
with courage and vigor and determination, we can by the end of 1952 be in
a position of much greater security. The way will be dangerous for the
years ahead, but if we put forth our best efforts this year—and next year—
we can be "over the hump" in our efforts to build strong defenses.

When we look at the record of the past year, 1951, we find important
things on both the credit and debit side of the ledger. We have made great
advances. At the same time we have run into new problems which must be
overcome.

Now let us look at the credit side first.

Peace depends upon the free nations sticking together, and making a combined effort to check aggression and prevent war. In this respect, 1951 was a year of great achievement.

In Korea the forces of the United Nations turned back the Chinese Communists invasion—and did it without widening the area of conflict. The action of the United Nations in Korea has been a powerful deterrent to a third world war. However, the situation in Korea remains very hazardous. The outcome of the armistice negotiation still remains uncertain.

In Indochina and Malaya, our aid has helped our allies to hold back the Communist advance, although there are signs of future trouble in that area.

In 1951 we strengthened the chances of peace in the Pacific region by the treaties with Japan and the defense arrangements with Australia, New Zealand, and the Philippines.

In Europe combined defense has become a reality. The free nations have created a real fighting force. This force is not yet as strong as it needs to be; but it is already a real obstacle to any attempt by hostile forces to sweep across Europe to the Atlantic.

In 1951 we also moved to strengthen the security of Europe by the agreement to bring Greece and Turkey into the North Atlantic Treaty.

The United Nations, the world's greatest hope for peace, has come through a year of trial stronger and more useful than ever. The free nations have stood together in blocking Communist attempts to tear up the charter.

At the present session of the United Nations in Paris, we, together with the British and the French, offered a plan to reduce and control all armaments under a foolproof inspection system. This is a concrete, practical proposal for disarmament.

But what happened? Vishinsky laughed at it. Listen to what he said: "I could hardly sleep at all last night. . . .I could not sleep because I kept laughing." The world will be a long time forgetting the spectacle of that fellow laughing at disarmament.

Disarmament is not a joke. Vishinsky's laughter met with shock and anger from all the people all over the world. And, as a result, Mr. Stalin's representative received orders to stop laughing and start talking.

If the Soviet leaders were to accept this proposal, it would lighten the burden of armaments, and permit the resources of the earth to be devoted to the good of mankind. But until the Soviet Union accepts a sound disarmament proposal, and joins in peaceful settlements, we have no choice except to build up our defenses.

During this past year we added more than a million men and women to our Armed Forces. The total is now nearly 3½ million. We have made rapid progress in the field of atomic weapons. We have turned out $16 billion worth of military supplies and equipment, three times as much as the year before.

Economic conditions in the country are good. There are 61 million people on the job; wages, farm incomes, and business profits are at high levels. Total production of goods and services in our country has increased 8 percent over last year—about twice the normal rate of growth.

Perhaps the most amazing thing about our economic progress is the way we are increasing our basic capacity to produce. For example, we are now in the second year of a 3-year program which will double our output of aluminum, increase our electric power supply by 40 percent, and increase our steel-making capacity by 15 percent. We can then produce 120 million tons of steel a year, as much as all the rest of the world put together.

This expansion will mean more jobs and higher standards of living for all of us in the years ahead. At the present time it means greater strength for us and for the rest of the free world in the fight for peace.

Now, I must turn to the debit side of the ledger for the past year.

The outstanding fact to note on the debit side of the ledger is that the Soviet Union, in 1951, continued to expand its military production and increase its already excessive military power.

It is true that the Soviets have run into increasing difficulties. Their hostile policies have awakened stern resistance among free men throughout the world. And behind the Iron Curtain the Soviet rule of force has created growing political and economic stresses in the satellite nations.

Nevertheless, the grim fact remains that the Soviet Union is increasing its armed might. It is still producing more war planes than the free nations. It has set off two more atomic explosions. The world still walks in the shadow of another world war.

And here at home, our defense preparations are far from complete.

During 1951 we did not make adequate progress in building up civil defense against atomic attack. This is a major weakness in our plans for peace, since inadequate civilian defense is an open invitation to a surprise attack. Failure to provide adequate civilian defense has the same effect as adding to the enemy's supply of atomic bombs.

In the field of defense production we have run into difficulties and delays in designing and producing the latest types of airplanes and tanks. Some machine tools and metals are still in extremely short supply.

In other free countries the defense buildup has created severe economic problems. It has increased inflation in Europe and has endangered the continued recovery of our allies.

In the Middle East political tensions and the oil controversy in Iran are keeping the region in a turmoil. In the Far East the dark threat of Communist imperialism still hangs over many nations.

This, very briefly, is the good side and the bad side of the picture.

Taking the good and bad together, we have made real progress this last year along the road to peace. We have increased the power and unity of the free world. And while we were doing this, we have avoided world war on the one hand, and appeasement on the other. This is a hard road to follow, but the events of the last year show that it is the right road to peace.

We cannot expect to complete the job overnight. The free nations may have to maintain for years the larger military forces needed to deter aggression. We must build steadily, over a period of years, toward political solidarity and economic progress among the free nations in all parts of the world.

Our task will not be easy; but if we go at it with a will, we can look forward to steady progress. On our side are all the great resources of freedom—the ideals of religion and democracy, the aspiration of people for a better life, and the industrial and technical power of a free civilization.

These advantages outweigh anything the slave world can produce. The only thing we can defeat is our own state of mind. We can lose if we falter.

The middle period of a great national effort like this is a very difficult time. The way seems long and hard. The goal seems far distant. Some people get discouraged. That is only natural.

But if there are any among us who think we ought to ease up in the fight for peace, I want to remind them of three things—just three things.

First: The threat of world war is still very real. We had one Pearl Harbor— let's not get caught off guard again. If you don't think the threat of Communist armies is real, talk to some of our men back from Korea.

Second: If the United States had to try to stand alone against a Soviet-dominated world, it would destroy the life we know and the ideals we hold dear. Our allies are essential to us, just as we are essential to them. The more shoulders there are to bear the burden the lighter that burden will be.

Third: The things we believe in most deeply are under relentless attack. We have the great responsibility of saving the basic moral and spiritual values of our civilization. We have started out well—with a program for peace that is unparalleled in history. If we believe in ourselves and the faith we profess, we will stick to that job until it is victoriously finished.

This is a time for courage, not for grumbling and mumbling.

Now, let us take a look at the things we have to do.

The thing that is uppermost in the minds of all of us is the situation in Korea. We must, and we will, keep up the fight there until we get the kind of armistice that will put an end to the aggression and protect the safety of our forces and the security of the Republic of Korea. Beyond that we shall continue to work for a settlement in Korea that upholds the principles of the United Nations.

We went into Korea because we knew that Communist aggression had to be met firmly if freedom was to be preserved in the world. We went into the fight to save the Republic of Korea, a free country, established under the United Nations. These are our aims. We will not give up until we attain them.

Meanwhile, we must continue to strengthen the forces of freedom throughout the world.

I hope the Senate will take early and favorable action on the Japanese peace treaty, on our security pacts with the Pacific countries, and on the agreement to bring Greece and Turkey into the North Atlantic Treaty.

We are also negotiating an agreement with the German Federal Republic under which it can play an honorable and equal part among nations and take its place in the defense of Western Europe.

But treaties and plans are only the skeleton of our de ense structure. The sinew and muscle of defense are the forces and equipment which must be provided.

In Europe we must go on helping our friends and allies to build up their military forces. The means we must send weapons in large volume to our European allies. I have directed that weapons for Europe be given a very high priority. Economic aid is necessary, too, to supply the margin of difference between success and failure in making Europe a strong partner in our joint defense.

In the long run we want to see Europe freed from any dependence on our aid. . . .

All these measures I have been talking about—measures to advance the well-being of our people—demonstrate to the world the forward movement of our free society.

This demonstration of the way free men govern themselves has a more powerful influence on the people of the world—on both sides of the Iron Curtain—than all the trick slogans and pie-in-the-sky promises of the Communists.

But our shortcomings, as well as our progress, are watched from abroad. And there is one shortcoming I want to speak about plainly.

Our kind of government above all others cannot tolerate dishonesty among public servants.

Some dishonest people worm themselves into almost every human organization. It is all the more shocking, however, when they make their way into a Government such as ours, which is based on the principle of justice for all. Such unworthy public servants must be weeded out. I intend to see to it that Federal employees who have been guilty of misconduct are punished for it. I also intend to see to it that the honest and hard-working great majority of our Federal employees are protected against partisan slander and malicious attack.

I have already made some recommendations to the Congress to help accomplish these purposes. I intend to submit further recommendations to this end. I will welcome the wholehearted cooperation of the Congress in this effort.

I also think that the Congress can do a great deal to strengthen confidence in our institutions by applying rigorous standards of moral integrity to its own operations, and by finding an effective way to control campaign expenditures, and by protecting the rights of individuals in congressional investigations.

To meet the crisis which now hangs over the world, we need many different kinds of strength—military, economic, political, and moral. And of all these, I am convinced that moral strength is the most vital.

When you come right down to it, it is the courage and the character of our Nation—and of each one of us as individuals—that will really decide how well we meet this challenge.

We are engaged in a great undertaking at home and abroad—the greatest in fact, that any nation has ever been privileged to embark upon. We are working night and day to bring peace to the world and to spread the democratic ideals of justice and self-government to all people. Our accomplishments are already remarkable. We ought to be full of pride in what we are doing, and full of confidence and hope in the outcome. No nation ever had greater resources, or greater energy, or nobler traditions to inspire it.

And yet, day in and day out, we see a long procession of timid and fearful men who wring their hands and cry out that we have lost the way, that we don't know what we are doing, that we are bound to fail. Some say we should give up the struggle for peace, and others say we should have a war and get it over with. That's a terrible statement. I had heard it made, but they want us to forget the great objective of preventing another world war—the objective for which our soldiers have been fighting in the hills of Korea.

If we are to be worthy of all that has been done for us by our soldiers in the field, we must be true to the ideals for which they are fighting. We must reject the counsels of defeat and despair. We must have the determination to complete the great work for which our men have laid down their lives.

In all we do, we should remember who we are and what we stand for. We are Americans. Our forefathers had far greater obstacles than we have, and much poorer chances of success. They did not lose heart, or turn aside from their goals. In the darkest of all winters in American history, at Valley Forge, George Washington said: "We must not, in so great a contest, expect to meet with nothing but sunshine." With that spirit they won their fight for freedom.

We must have that same faith and vision. In the great contest in which we are engaged today, we cannot expect to have fair weather all the way. But it is a contest just as important for this country and for all men, as the desperate struggle that George Washington fought through to victory.

Let us prove, again, that we are not merely sunshine patriots and summer soldiers. Let us go forward, trusting in the God of Peace, to win the goals we seek.

ON THE GOVERNMENT OPERATION OF THE STEEL MILLS
April 9, 1952

*When the steel companies refused to abide by a wage Media-
tion Board award of higher wages to workers without a rise in
steel prices, Truman, under emergency powers, seized the steel
mills.*

To the Congress of the United States:

The Congress is undoubtedly aware of the recent events which have
taken place in connection with the management-labor dispute in the steel
industry. These events culminated in the action which was taken last night
to provide for temporary operation of the steel mills by the Government.

I took this action with the utmost reluctance. The idea of Government
operation of the steel mills is thoroughly distasteful to me and I want to see
it ended as soon as possible. However, in the situation which confronted
me yesterday, I felt that I could make no other choice. The other alternatives
appeared to be even worse—so much worse that I could not accept them.

One alternative would have been to permit a shutdown in the steel industry. The effects of such a shutdown would have been so immediate and
damaging with respect to our efforts to support our armed forces and to
protect our national security that it made this alternative unthinkable.

The only way that I know of, other than Government operation, by
which a steel shutdown could have been avoided was to grant the demands
of the steel industry for a large price increase. I believed and the officials in
charge of our stabilization agencies believed that this would have wrecked
our stabilization program. I was unwilling to accept the incalculable damage which might be done to our country by following such a course.

Accordingly, it was my judgment that Government operation of the
steel mills for a temporary period was the least undesirable of the course of
action which lay open. In the circumstances, I believed it to be, and now believe it to be, my duty and within my powers as President to follow that
course of action.

It may be that Congress will deem some other course to be wiser. It may
be that the Congress will feel we should give in to the demands of the steel
industry for an exorbitant price increase and take the consequences so far
as resulting inflation is concerned.

It may be that the Congress will feel the Government should try to force
the steel workers to continue to work for the steel companies for another
long period without a contract, even though the steel workers have already
voluntarily remained at work without a contract for 100 days in an effort to
reach an orderly settlement of their differences with management.

It may even be that the Congress will feel that we should permit a shutdown of the steel industry, although that would immediately endanger the safety of our fighting forces abroad and weaken the whole structure of our national security.

I do not believe the Congress will favor any of these courses of action, but that is a matter for the Congress to determine.

It may be, on the other hand, that the Congress will wish to pass legislation establishing specific terms and conditions with reference to the operation of the steel mills by the Government. Sound legislation of this character might be very desirable.

On the basis of the facts that are known to me at this time, I do not believe that immediate Congressional action is essential; but I would, of course, be glad to cooperate in developing any legislative proposals which the Congress may wish to consider.

If the Congress does not deem it necessary to act at this time, I shall continue to do all that is within my power to keep the steel industry operating and at the same time make every effort to bring about a settlement of the dispute so the mills can be returned to their private owners as soon as possible.

HARRY S TRUMAN

VETO OF McCARRAN-WALTER IMMIGRATION ACT
June 25, 1952

*Truman vetoed this bill on Constitutional and other grounds,
but Congress passed it over his veto.*

To the House of Representatives:

I return herewith, without my approval, H.R. 5678, the proposed Immigration and Nationality Act.

In outlining my objections to this bill, I want to make it clear that it contains certain provisions that meet with my approval. This is a long and complex piece of legislation. It has 164 separate sections, some with more than 40 subdivisions. It presents a difficult problem of weighing the good against the bad, and arriving at a judgment on the whole.

H.R. 5678 is an omnibus bill which would revise and codify all of our laws relating to immigration, naturalization, and nationality.

A general revision and modernization of these laws unquestionably is needed and long overdue, particularly with respect to immigration. But this bill would not provide us with an immigration policy adequate for the present world situation. Indeed, the bill, taking all its provisions together, would be a step backward and not a step forward. In view of the crying need for reform in the field of immigration, I deeply regret that I am unable to approve H.R. 5678.

In recent years our immigration policy has become a matter of major national concern. Long dormant questions about the effect of our immigration laws now assume first-rate importance. What we do in the field of immigration and naturalization is vital to the continued growth and internal development of the United States—to the economic and social strength of our country—which is the core of the defense of the free world. Our immigration policy is equally, if not more, important to the conduct of our foreign relations and to our responsibilities of moral leadership in the struggle for world peace.

In one respect, this bill recognizes the great international significance of our immigration and naturalization policy, and takes a step to improve existing laws. All racial bars to naturalization would be removed, and at least some minimum immigration quota would be afforded to each of the free nations of Asia.

I have long urged that racial or national barriers to naturalization be abolished. This was one of the recommendations in my civil-rights message to the Congress on February 2, 1948. On February 19, 1951, the House of Representatives unanimously passed a bill to carry it out.

But now this most desirable provision comes before me embedded in a mass of legislation which would perpetuate injustices of long standing against many other nations of the world, hamper the efforts we are making to rally the men of the east and west alike to the cause of freedom, and intensify the repressive and inhumane aspects of our immigration procedures. The price is too high and, in good conscience, I cannot agree to pay it. . . .

In addition to removing racial bars to naturalization, the bill would permit American women citizens to bring their alien husbands to this country as nonquota immigrants, and enable alien husbands of resident women aliens to come in under the quota in a preferred status. These provisions would be a step toward preserving the integrity of the family under our immigration laws, and are clearly desirable. . . .

But these few improvements are heavily outweighted by other provisions of the bill which retain existing defects in our laws, and add many undesirable new features.

The bill would continue, practically without change, the national origins quota system, which was enacted into law in 1924, and put into effect in 1929. This quota system—always based upon assumptions at variance with our American ideals—is long since out of date and more than ever unrealistic in the face of present world conditions.

This system hinders us in dealing with current immigration problems, and is a constant handicap in the conduct of our foreign relations. As I stated in my message to Congress on March 24, 1952, on the need for an emergency program of immigration from Europe:

> "Our present quota system is not only inadequate to meet present emergency needs, it is also an obstacle to the development of an enlightened and satisfactory immigration policy for the long-run future."

The inadequacy of the present quota system has been demonstrated since the end of the war, when we were compelled to restore to emergency legislation to admit displaced persons. If the quota system remains unchanged, we shall be compelled to resort to similar emergency legislation again, in order to admit any substantial portion of the refugees from communism or the victims of overcrowding in Europe.

With the idea of quotas in general there is no quarrel. Some numerical limitation must be set, so that immigration will be within our capacity to absorb. But the over-all limitation of numbers imposed by the national origins quota system is too small for our needs today, and the country by country limitations create a pattern that is insulting to large numbers of our finest citizens, irritating to our allies abroad, and foreign to our purposes and ideals.

The over-all quota limitation, under the law of 1924, restricted annual immigration to approximately 150,000. This was about one-seventh of 1 percent of our total population in 1920. Taking into account the growth in population since 1920, the law now allows us but one-tenth of 1 percent of our total population. And since the largest national quotas are only partly used, the number actually coming in has been in the neighborhood of one-fifteenth of 1 percent. This is far less than we must have in the years ahead to keep up with the growing needs of our Nation for manpower to maintain the strength and vigor of our economy.

The greatest vice of the present quota system, however, is that it discriminates, deliberately and intentionally, against many of the peoples of the world. The purpose behind it was to cut down and virtually eliminate immigration to this country from southern and eastern Europe. A theory was invented to rationalize this objective. The theory was that in order to be readily assimilable, European immigrants should be admitted in proportion to the numbers of persons of their respective national stocks already here as shown by the census of 1920. Since Americans of English, Irish, and German descent were most numerous, immigrants of those three nationalities got the lion's share—more than two-thirds—of the total quota. The remaining third was divided up among all the other nations given quotas.

The desired effect was obtained. Immigration from the newer sources of Southern and Eastern Europe was reduced to a trickle. The quotas allotted to England and Ireland remained largely unused, as was intended. Total quota immigration fell to a half or a third—and sometimes even less—of the annual limit of 154,000. People from such countries as Greece, or Spain, or Latvia were virtually deprived of any opportunity to come here at all, simply because Greeks or Spaniards or Latvians had not come here before 1920 in any substantial numbers.

The idea behind this discriminatory policy was to put it badly, that Americans with English or Irish names were better people and better citizens than Americans with Italian or Greek or Polish names. It was thought that people of West European origin made better citizens than Rumanians or Yugoslavs or Ukrainians or Hungarians or Balts or Austrians. Such a concept is utterly unworthy of our traditions and our ideals. It violates the great political doctrine of the Declaration of Independence that "all men are created equal." It denies the humanitarian creed inscribed beneath the Statue of Liberty proclaiming to all nations, "Give me your tired, your poor, your huddled masses yearning to breathe free."

It repudiates our basic religious concepts, our beliefs in the brotherhood of man, and in the words of St. Paul that "there is neither Jew nor Greek, there is neither bond nor free, . . . for ye are all one in Christ Jesus."

The basis of this quota system was false and unworthy in 1924. It is even worse now. At the present time this quota system keeps out the very people we want to bring in. It is incredible to me that, in this year of 1952, we should again be enacting into law such a slur on the patriotism, the capacity, and the decency of a large part of our citizenry. . . .

The time to shake off this dead weight of past mistakes is now. The time to develop a decent policy of immigration—a fitting instrument for our foreign

policy and a true reflection of the ideals we stand for, at home and abroad—
is now. In my earlier message on immigration, I tried to explain to the Congress that the situation we face in immigration is an emergency—that is must
be met promptly. I have pointed out that in the last few years, we have
blazed a new trail in immigration, through our displaced persons program.
Through the combined efforts of the Government and private agencies,
working together not to keep people out, but to bring qualified people in,
we summoned our resources of good will and human feeling to meet the
task. In this program we have found better techniques to meet the immigration problems of the 1950's.

None of this fruitful experience of the last 3 years is reflected in this bill
before me. None of the crying human needs of this time of trouble is recognized in this bill. But it is not too late. The Congress can remedy these defects, and it can adopt legislation to meet the most critical problems before
adjournment. . . .

I now wish to turn to the other provisions of the bill, those dealing with the
qualifications of aliens and immigrants for admission, with the administration of the laws, and with problems of naturalization and nationality. In
these provisions, too, I find objections that preclude my signing this bill.

The bill would make it even more difficult to enter our country. Our
resident aliens would be more easily separated from homes and families
under grounds of deportation, both new and old, which would specifically
be made retroactive. Admission to our citizenship would be made more difficult; expulsion from our citizenship would be made easier. Certain rights
of native-born, first-generation Americans would be limited. All our citizens
returning from abroad would be subjected to serious risk of unreasonable
invasions of privacy. Seldom has a bill exhibited the distrust evidenced here
for citizens and aliens alike—at a time when we need unity at home and the
confidence of our friends abroad. . . .

I am asked to approve the reenactment of highly objectionable provisions
now contained in the Internal Security Act of 1950—a measure passed over
my veto shortly after the invasion of South Korea. Some of these provisions
would empower the Attorney General to deport any alien who has engaged
or has had a purpose to engage in activities "prejudicial to the public interest" or "subversive to the national security." No standards or definitions are
provided to guide discretion in the exercise of powers so sweeping. To punish
undefined "activities" departs from traditional American insistence on
established standards of guilt. To punish an undefined "purpose" is thought
control. . . .

This illustrates the fundamental error of these immigration and naturalization provisions. It is easy to see that they are hasty and ill-considered. But
far more significant—and far more dangerous—is their apparent underlying
purpose. Instead of trying to encourage the free movement of people, sub-

ject only to the real requirements of national security, these provisions attempt to bar movement to anyone who is, or once was, associated with ideas we dislike and, in the process, they would succeed in barring many people whom it would be to our advantage to admit. . . .

STATE OF THE UNION MESSAGE
January 7, 1953

This last state of the Union Address was essentially a summary of Truman's eight years as President.

To the Congress of the United States:

I have the honor to report to the Congress on the state of the Union.

This is the eighth such report that, as President, I have been privileged to present to you and to the country. On previous occasions, it has been my custom to set forth proposals for legislative action in the coming year. But that is not my purpose today. The presentation of a legislative program falls properly to my successor, not to me, and I would not infringe upon his responsibility to chart the forward course. Instead, I wish to speak of the course we have been following the past eight years and the position at which we have arrived.

In just two weeks, General Eisenhower will be inaugurated as President of the United States and I will resume—most gladly—my place as a private citizen of this Republic. The Presidency last changed hands eight years ago this coming April. That was a tragic time: a time of grieving for President Roosevelt—the great and gallant human being who had been taken from us; a time of unrelieved anxiety to his successor, thrust so suddenly into the complexities and burdens of the Presidential office.

Not so this time. This time we see the normal transition under our democratic system. One President, at the conclusion of his term, steps back to private life; his successor, chosen by the people, begins his tenure of the office. And the Presidency of the United States continues to function without a moment's break.

Since the election, I have done my best to assure that the transfer from one Administration to another shall be smooth and orderly. From General Eisenhower and his associates, I have had friendly and understanding collaboration in this endeavor. I have not sought to thrust upon him—nor has he sought to take—the responsibility which must be mine until twelve o'clock noon on January twentieth. But together, I hope and believe we have found means whereby the incoming President can obtain the full and detailed information he will need to assume the responsibility the moment he takes the oath of office.

The President-elect is about to take up the greatest burdens, the most compelling responsibilities, given to any man. And I, with you and all Americans, wish for him all possible success in undertaking the tasks that will so soon be his.

What are these tasks? The President is Chief of State, elected representative of all the people, national spokesman for them and to them. He is Com-

mander-in-Chief of our armed forces. He is charged with the conduct of our
foreign relations. He is Chief Executive of the Nation's largest civilian organization. He must select and nominate all top officials of the Executive
Branch and all Federal judges. And on the legislative side, he has the obligation and the opportunity to recommend, and to approve or veto legislation. Besides all this, it is to him that a great political party turns naturally
for leadership, and that, too, he must provide as President.

This bundle of burdens is unique; there is nothing else like it on the face
of the earth. Each task could be a full-time job. Together, they would be a
tremendous undertaking in the easiest of times.

But our times are not easy; they are hard—as hard and complex, perhaps
as any in our history. Now, the President not only has to carry on these
tasks in such a way that our democracy may grow and flourish and our
people prosper, but he also has to lead the whole free world in overcoming
the communist menace—and all this under the shadow of the atomic bomb.

This is a huge challenge to the human being who occupies the Presidential
office. But it is not a challenge to him alone, for in reality he cannot meet it
alone. The challenge runs not just to him but to his whole Administration,
to the Congress, to the country.

Ultimately, no President can master his responsibilities, save as his fellow citizens—indeed, the whole people—comprehend the challenge of our
times and move, with him, to meet it.

It has been my privilege to hold the Presidental office for nearly eight
years now, and much has been done in which I take great pride. But this is
not personal pride. It is pride in the people, in the Nation. It is pride in the
political system and our form of government—balky sometimes, mechani-
cally deficient perhaps, in many ways—but enormously alive and vigorous;
able through these years to keep the Republic on the right course, rising
to the great occasions, accomplishing the essentials, meeting the basic
challenge of our times.

There have been misunderstandings and controversies these past eight
years, but through it all the President of the United States has had the measure of support and understanding without which no man could sustain
the burdens of the Presidential office, or hope to discharge its responsibilities.

For this I am profoundly grateful—grateful to my associates in the Executive Branch—most of them non-partisan civil servants; grateful—despite
our disagreements—to the Members of the Congress on both sides of the
aisle; grateful especially to the American people, the citizens of the Republic,
governors of us all.

We are still so close to recent controversies that some of us may find it
hard to understand the accomplishments of these past eight years. But the
accomplishments are real and very great, not as the President's, not as the
Congress', but as the achievements of our country and all the people in it.

Let me remind you of some of the things we have done since I first assumed my duties as President of the United States.

I took the oath of office on April 12, 1945. In May of that same year, the Nazis surrendered. Then, in July, that great white flash of light, man-made at Alamogordo, heralded swift and final victory in World War II—and opened the doorway to the atomic age.

Consider some of the great questions that were posed for us by sudden, total victory in World War II. Consider also, how well we as a Nation have responded.

Would the American economy collapse, after the war? That was one question. Would there be another depression here—a repetition of 1921 or 1929? The free world feared and dreaded it. The communists hoped for it and built their policies upon that hope.

We answered that question—answered it with a resounding "no."

Our economy has grown tremendously. Free enterprise has flourished as never before. Sixty-two million people are now gainfully employed, compared with 51 million seven years ago. Private businessmen and farmers have invested more than 200 billion dollars in new plant and equipment since the end of World War II. Prices have risen further than they shoud have done— but incomes, by and large, have risen even more, so that real living standards are now considerably higher than seven years ago. . . .

War has changed its shape and its dimension. It cannot now be a "stage" in the development of anything save ruin for your regime and your homeland.

I do not know how much time may elapse before the communist rulers bring themselves to recognize this truth. But when they do, they will find us eager to reach understandings that will protect the world from the danger it faces today.

It is no wonder that some people wish that we had never succeeded in splitting the atom. But atomic power, like any other force of nature, is not evil in itself. Properly used, it is an instrumentality for human betterment. As a source of power, as a tool of scientific inquiry, it has untold possibilities. We are already making good progress in the constructive use of atomic power. We could do much more if we were free to concentrate on its peaceful uses exclusively.

Atomic power will be with us all the days of our lives. We cannot legislate it out of existence. We cannot ignore the dangers or the benefits it offers.

I believe that man can harness the forces of the atom to work for the improvement of the lot of human beings everywhere. That is our goal. As a nation, as a people, we must understand this problem, we must handle this new force wisely through our democratic processes. Above all, we must strive, in all earnestness and good faith, to bring it under effective international control. To do this will require much wisdom and patience and firmness. The awe-inspiring responsibility in this field now falls on a new Administration and a new Congress. I will give them my support, as I am sure all our citizens will, in whatever constructive steps they may take to make this newest of man's discoveries a source of good and not of ultimate destruction.

We cannot tell when or whether the attitude of the Soviet rulers may change. We do not know how long it may be before they show a willingness to negotiate effective control of atomic energy and honorable settlements of other world problems. We cannot measure how deep-rooted are the Kremlin's illusions about us. We can be sure, however, that the rulers of the communist world will not change their basic objectives lightly or soon.

The communist rulers have a sense of time about these things wholly unlike our own. We tend to divide our future into short spans, like the two-year life of this Congress, or the four years of the next Presidential term. They seem to think and plan in terms of generations. And there is, therefore, no easy, short-run way to make them see that their plans cannot prevail.

This means there is ahead of us a long hard test of strength and stamina, between the free world and the communist domain—our politics and our economy, our science and technology against the best they can do—our liberty against their slavery—our voluntary concert of free nations against their forced amalgam of "people's republics"—our stategy against their strategy—our nerve against their nerve.

Above all, this is a test of the will and the steadiness of the people of the United States.

There has been no challenge like this in the history of our Republic. We are called upon to rise to the occasion, as no people before us.

What is required of us is not easy. The way we must learn to live, the world we have to live in, cannot be so pleasant, safe or simple as most of us have known before, or confidently hoped to know.

Already we have had to sacrifice a number of accustomed ways of working and of living, much nervous energy, material resources, even human life. Yet if one thing is certain in our future, it is that more sacrifice still lies ahead.

Were we to grow discouraged now, were we to weaken and slack off, the whole structure we have built, these past eight years, would come apart and fall away. Never then, no matter by what stringent means, could our free world regain the ground, the time, the sheer momentum lost by such a move. There can and should be changes and improvements in our programs, to meet new situations, serve new needs. But to desert the spirit of our basic policies, to step back from them now, would surely start the free world's slide toward the darkness that the communists have prophesied—toward the moment for which they watch and wait.

If we value our freedom and our way of life and want to see them safe, we must meet the challenge and accept its implications, stick to our guns and carry out our policies.

I have set out the basic conditions, as I see them, under which we have been working in the world, and the nature of our basic policies. What, then, of the future? The answer, I believe, is this: As we continue to confound Soviet expectations, as our world grows stronger, more united, more attractive to men on both sides of the iron curtain, then inevitably there will come a time of change within the communist world. We do not know how that change will come about, whether by deliberate decision in the Kremlin, by coup d'etat, by revolution, by defection of satellites, or perhaps by some unforeseen combination of factors such as these.

But if the communist rulers understand they cannot win by war, and if we frustrate their attempts to win by subversion, it is not too much to expect their world to change its character, moderate its aims, become more realistic and less implacable, and recede from the cold war they began.

Do not be deceived by the strong face, the look of monolithic power that the communist dictators wear before the outside world. Remember their power has no basis in consent. Remember they are so afraid of the free world's ideas and ways of life, they do not dare to let their people know about them. Think of the massive effort they put forth to try to stop our Campaign of Truth from reaching their people with its message of freedom.

The masters of the Kremlin live in fear their power and position would collapse were their own people to acquire knowledge, information, comprehension about our free society. Their world has many elements of strength, but this one fatal flaw: the weakness represented by their iron curtain and their police state. Surely, a social order at once so insecure and so fearful, must ultimately lose its competition with our free society.

All these measures I have been talking about—measures to advance the well-being of our people—demonstrate to the world the forward movement of our free society.

This demonstration of the way free men govern themselves has a more powerful influence on the people of the world—on both sides of the Iron Curtain—than all the trick slogans and pie-in-the-sky promises of the Communists.

But our shortcomings, as well as our progress, are watched from abroad. And there is one shortcoming I want to speak about plainly.

Our kind of government above all othjs cannot tolerate dishonesty among public servants.

Some dishonest people worm themselves into almost every human organization. It is all the more shocking, however, when they make their way into a Government such as ours, which is based on the principle of justice for all. Such unworthy public servants must be weeded out. I intend to see to it that Federal employees who have been guilty of misconduct are punished for it. I also intend to see to it that the honest and hard-working great majority of our Federal employees are protected against partisan slander and malicious attack.

I have already made some recommendations to the Congress to help accomplish these purposes. I intend to submit further recommendations to this end. I will welcome the wholehearted cooperation of the Congress in this effort . . .

Let all of us pause now, think back, consider carefully the meaning of our national experience. Let us draw comfort from it and faith, and confidence in our future as Americans.

The Nation's business is never finished. The basic questions we have been dealing with, these eight years past, present themselves anew. That is the way of our society. Circumstances change and current questions take on different forms, new complications, year by year. But underneath, the great issues remain the same— prosperity, welfare, human rights, effective democracy, and above all, peace.

Now we turn to the inaugural of our new President. And in the great work he is called upon to do he will have need for the support of a united people, a confident people, with firm faith in one another and in our common cause. I pledge him my support as a citizen of our Republic, and I ask you to give him yours.

To him, to you, to all my fellow citizens, I say, Godspeed.

May God bless our country and our cause.

                                        HARRY S TRUMAN

FAREWELL ADDRESS TO THE AMERICAN PEOPLE
January 15, 1953

In this last message to the nation, Truman defended his administration, and talked of the difficulties of the office of President.

My fellow Americans:

I am happy to have this opportunity to talk to you once more before I leave the White House.

Next Tuesday, General Eisenhower will be inaugurated as President of the United States. A short time after the new President takes his oath of office, I will be on the train going back home to Independence, Missouri. I will once again be a plain, private citizen of this great Republic.

That is as it should be. Inauguration Day will be a great demonstration of our democratic process. I am glad to be a part of it—glad to wish General Eisenhower all possible success, as he begins his term—glad the whole world will have a chance to see how simply and how peacefully our American system transfers the vast power of the Presidency from my hands to his. It is a good object lesson in democracy. I am very proud of it. And I know you are, too.

During the last 2 months I have done my best to make this transfer an orderly one. I have talked with my successor on the affairs of the country, both foreign and domestic, and my Cabinet officers have talked with their successors. I want to say that General Eisenhower and his associates have cooperated fully in this effort. Such an orderly transfer from one party to another has never taken place before in our history. I think a real precedent has been set.

In speaking to you tonight, I have no new revelations to make—no political statements—no policy announcements. There are simply a few things in my heart that I want to say to you. I want to say "goodby" and "thanks for your help." And I want to talk to you a little while about what has happened since I became your President.

I am speaking to you from the room where I have worked since April 12, 1945. This is the President's office in the West Wing of the White House. This is the desk where I have signed most of the papers that embodied the decisions I have made as President. It has been the desk of many Presidents, and will be the desk of many more.

Since I became President, I have been to Europe, Mexico, Canada, Brazil, Puerto Rico, and the Virgin Islands—Wake Island and Hawaii. I have visited almost every State in the Union. I have traveled 135,000 miles by air, 77,000 by rail, and 17,000 by ship. But the mail always followed me, and wherever I happened to be, that's where the office of the President was.

The greatest part of the President's job is to make decisions—big ones and small ones, dozens of them almost every day. The papers may circulate around the Government for a while but they finally reach this desk. And then, there's no place else for them to go. The President—whoever he is—has to decide. He can't pass the buck to anybody. No one else can do the deciding for him. That's his job.

That's what I've been doing here in this room, for almost 8 years. And over in the main part of the White House, there's a study on the second floor—a room much like this one—where I have worked at night and early in the morning on the papers I couldn't get to at the office.

Of course, for more than 3 years Mrs. Truman and I were not living in the White House. We were across the street in the Blair House. That was when the White House almost fell down on us and had to be rebuilt. I had a study over at the Blair House, too, but living in the Blair House was not as convenient as living in the White House. The Secret Service wouldn't let me walk across the street, so I had to get in a car every morning to cross the street to the White House office, again at noon to go to the Blair House for lunch, again to go back to the office after lunch, and finally take an automobile at night to return to the Blair House. Fantastic, isn't it? But necessary, so my guards thought—and they are the bosses on such matters as that.

Now, of course, we're back in the White House. It is in very good condition, and General Eisenhower will be able to take up his residence in the house and work right here. That will be much more convenient for him, and I'm very glad the renovation job was all completed before his term began.

Your new President is taking office in quite different circumstances than when I became President 8 years ago. On April 12, 1945, I had been presiding over the Senate in my capacity as Vice President. When the Senate recessed about 5 o'clock in the afternoon, I walked over to the office of the speaker of the House, Mr. Rayburn, to discuss pending legislation. As soon as I arrived, I was told that Mr. Early, one of President Roosevelt's secretaries, wanted me to call. I reached Mr. Early, and he told me to come to the White House as quickly as possible, to enter by way of the Pennsylvania Avenue entrance, and to come to Mrs. Roosevelt's study.

When I arrived, Mrs. Roosevelt told me the tragic news, and I felt the shock that all of you felt a little later—when the word came over the radio and appeared in the newspapers. President Roosevelt had died. I offered to do anything I could for Mrs. Roosevelt, and then I asked the Secretary of State to call the Cabinet together.

At 7:09 p.m. I was sworn in as President by Chief Justice Stone in the Cabinet Room.

Things were happening fast in those days. The San Francisco conference to organize the United Nations had been called for April 25th. I was asked if that meeting would go forward. I announced that it would. That was my first decision.

After attending President Roosevelt's funeral, I went to the Hall of the House of Representatives and told a joint session of the Congress that I would carry on President Roosevelt's policies.

On May 7th, Germany surrendered. The announcement was made on May 8th, my 61st birthday.

Mr. Churchill called me shortly after that and wanted a meeting with me and Prime Minister Stalin of Russia. Later on, a meeting was agreed upon, and Churchill, Stalin, and I met at Potsdam in Germany.

Meanwhile, the first atomic explosion took place out in the New Mexico desert.

The war against Japan was still going on. I made the decision that the atomic bomb had to be used to end it. I made that decision in the conviction it would save hundreds of thousands of lives—Japanese as well as American. Japan surrendered, and we were faced with the huge problem of bringing the troops home and reconverting the economy from war to peace.

All these things happened within just a little over 4 months—from April to August 1945. I tell you this to illustrate the tremendous scope of the work your President has to do.

And all these emergencies and all the developments to meet them have required the President to put in long hours—usually 17 hours a day, with no payment for overtime. I sign my name, on the average, 600 times a day, see and talk to hundreds of people every month, shake hands with thousands every year, and still carry on the business of the largest going concern in the whole world. There is no job like it on the face of the earth—in the power which is concentrated here at this desk, and in the responsibility and difficulty of the decisions. . . .

We have made progress in spreading the blessing of American life to all of our people. There has been a tremendous awakening of the American conscience on the great issues of civil rights—equal economic opportunities, equal rights of citizenship, and equal educational opportunities for all our people, whatever their race or religion or status of birth.

So, as I empty the drawers of this desk, and as Mrs. Truman and I leave the White House, we have no regret. We feel we have done our best in the public service. I hope and believe we have contributed to the welfare of this Nation and to the peace of the world.

When Franklin Roosevelt died, I felt there must be a million men better qualified than I, to take up the Presidental task. But the work was mine to do, and I had to do it. And I have tried to give it everything that was in me.

Through all of it, through all the years that I have worked here in this room, I have been well aware I did not really work alone—that you were working with me.

No President could ever hope to lead our country, or to sustain the burdens of this office, save as the people helped with their support. I have had that support. I have had that help—you have given me that support—on all our great essential undertakings to build the free world's strength and keep the peace.

Those are the big things. Those are the things we have done together.

For that I shall be grateful, always.

And now, the time has come for me to say good night—and God bless you all.

BIBLIOGRAPHICAL AIDS

Not enough time has elapsed nor has sufficient research been done to permit historians to pass considered judgment on the presidency of Harry S Truman. Yet, the literature on the Truman administration is constantly growing and is already quite large. There is a considerable amount of documents concerned with the Truman administration—public correspondence,printed reports, mimeographed statements and speeches, some private correspondence—that are available almost anywhere. The Harry S Truman Memorial Library at Independence, Missouri, claims five million papers on the Presidency. The Library of Congress contains most of this same material. However, the bulk of Truman's private correspondence, the working papers, notes, and other documents relating to major policy matters are located in Mr. Truman's wing of the library at Independence, and are not available to the historian, let alone the public. They have not been examined nor catalogued by the Library's director. Nevertheless, there is a huge amount of material available to students, and the general public. Probably the best summary of events and discussion of the bibliography on Truman's government is Richard Kirkendall's *The Truman Period as a Research Field, Missouri, 1967*. In addition, the papers in the Library of Congress are indexed and available on microfilm.

SOURCE MATERIALS

Congressional Record, Washington, D.C., 1945-1953.

Department of States. *Bulletin.* Washington, D.C., 1945-1953.

Department of State. *Foreign Relations Series,* 1945-1953. Washington, D.C., 1945-1953.

Presidential Papers Microfilm: *Harry S Truman.* Washington, D.C., 1967.

Public Papers of the Presidents: Harry S Truman, 1945-1953. 8 vols. Washington, D.C., 1961-1967.

Senate Foreign Relations Committee. *Decade of American Foreign Policy: Basic Documents.* Eighty-First Congress, first session, Senate Document 123.

Truman, Harry S. *Memoirs.* 2 vols. Garden City, Long Island 1955.*

BIOGRAPHIES

Bundschu, Henry A. *Harry S. Truman—The Missourian.* New York, 1948. Is rather short, covering up to, but not including the election of 1948.

Daniels, Jonathan. *The Man of Independence.* Philadelphia, 1950. Points up Truman's love of history, and is fairly complete as far as it goes, although administrative history is glossed over rather quickly.

Dayton, Eldorous L. *Give 'Em Hell, Harry.* New York, 1956. Colorful, robust study. Contains a good deal of information, but not of the scholarly variety.

Helm, William P. *Harry Truman.* New York, 1947. This biography is limited, carrying the Truman story up to 1947. Yet, it does contain valuable material on Truman's early career.

Hillman, William. *Mr. President.* New York, 1952. A very short, superficial view of Truman, containing excerpts from speeches, letters, etc. Excellent illustrations.

McNaughton, Frank, and Hehmeyer, Walter. *This Man Truman.* New York, 1945. A highly partisan study of Truman's life and character up to his taking over the presidency.

Phillips, Cabell. *The Truman Presidency.* New York, 1966. This is an exhaustive biography of the two Truman administrations. Well documented, objective and quite perceptive.

Powell, Gene. *Tom's Boy Harry.* New York, 1948. Includes much detail on Truman's early years, especially his rise in the political arena and his relationship with Thomas J. Pendergast of Kansas City.

Schauffler, Edward R. *Harry Truman—Son of the Soil.* New York, 1947. This popularized biography is thoroughly readable, but ends early in 1947.

Steinberg, Alfred. *The Man from Missouri: The Life and Times of Harry S. Truman.* New York, 1962. This biography is about the best scholarly history of the Truman administration.

GENERAL WORKS

Agar, Herbert. *The Price of Power.* Chicago, 1957. This book briefly discusses Truman's presidency.*

Barck, Oscar T. *A History of the United States since 1945.* New York, 1965. This survey affords a useful starting point for the student.*

Bernstein, Barton J. and Matusow, Allen J. eds. *The Truman Administration: A Documentary History.* New York, 1966. A vivid, narrative story, this book tells through transcripts of hearings, correspondence, memoranda, diaries, and other sources, the lively, often controversial story of the Truman era.

Clemens, Cyril, ed. *Truman Speaks.* New York, 1946. A compilation of Truman speeches and public correspondence through 1946.

Freidel, Frank. *America in the Twentieth Century.* New York, 1960. Truman's eight years in the White House receive considerable attention in this excellent book.

Goldman, Eric F. *The Crucial Decade—and After, America 1945-1960.* New York, 1960. An excellent survey of this period, done in a scholarly manner with perceptive insights into the great issues of these years.*

Graebner, Norman. *Cold War Diplomacy.* New York, 1962. One of the most available and readable studies on post-war foreign policy.*

Johnson, Walter. *1600 Pennsylvania Avenue: Presidents and People Since 1929.* Boston, 1960. This is a very useful, but brief, study, covering the eight years of the Truman administration in an interesting way.*

Lukacs, John. *History of the Cold War.* New York, 1961. A penetrating study of the origins and development of the cold war with scholarly coverage of Truman's role in this period.

Spanier, John *American Foreign Policy Since World War II.* New York, 1962. A very useful introduction to foreign affairs covering this aspect of history up to 1961.*

Spanier, John. *The Truman-MacArthur Controversy and the Korean War.* New York, 1962. A very good account of this controversial and important aspect of the Truman Adminstration.*

For students wishing to read further in the various areas of the Truman Administrations, the following selective bibliography will serve as a beginning.

THE A-BOMB DECISION

Alperowitz, Gar. *Atomic Diplomacy: Hiroshima and Potsdam.* New York, 1965.

Butow, Robert. *Japan's Decision to Surrender.* Stanford, 1954.

Churchill, Winston. *The Second World War,* Vol. II,. Boston, 1953.*

Feis, Herbert. *Between War and Peace: The Potsdam Conference,* Princeton, 1960.

Giovannitti, Len and Freed, Frederick. *The Decision to Drop the Bomb.* New York, 1960.

Groves, Leslie. *Now It Can Be Told: The Story of the Manhattan Project.* New York, 1962.

Morton, Louis. "The Decision to Use the Atomic Bomb," in *Command Decisions,* ed. Kent Roberts Greenfield. Washington, D.C., 1958.

Strauss, Lewis. *Men and Decisions.* New York, 1962.

INFLATION AND POLITICS

Abbot, Charles, *The Federal Debt: Structure and Impact,* New York, 1953.

Abels, Jules. *The Truman Scandals.* New York, 1956.

Bailey, Stephen. *Congress Makes a Law: The Story Behind the Employment Act of 1946.* New York, 1950.

Coffin, Tris. *Missouri Compromise.* Boston, 1947.

Holman, A.E. *United States Fiscal Policy, 1945-1959.* New York, 1961.

Lubell, Samuel, *The Future of American Politics.* New York, 1952.*

Seidman, Joel. *American Labor from Defense to Reconversion.* Chicago, 1953.

Somers, Herman. *Presidential Agency: The Office of War Mobilization and Reconversion.* Cambridge, Mass. 1950.

THE FAIR DEAL

Allen, Robert and Shannon, William. *The Truman-Merry-Go-Round.* New York, 1950.

Bell, Daniel, ed. *The New American Right.* New York, 1955.

Blaustein, Albert and Ferguson, Clyde. *Desegregation and the Law.* New Brunswick, 1957.

Carr, Robert. *The Federal Protection of Civil Rights.* Ithaca, 1947.

Davies, Richard. *Housing Reform During the Truman Administration,* Columbia, Mo., 1966.

Kesselman, Louis. *The Social Politics of F.E.P.C.* Chapel Hill, 1948.

Konvitz, Milton, *The Constitution and Civil Rights.* New York, 1947.

Longaker, Richard. *The Presidency and Individual Liberty.* Ithaca, 1961.

Millis, Harry and Brown, Emily. *From the Wagner Act to Taft-Hartley.* Chicago, 1950.

President's Committee on Civil Rights. *To Secure These Rights,* Washington, D.C., 1947.

Schmidt, Karl. *Henry Wallace: Quixotic Crusader.* Syracuse, 1960.

Truman, Harry S. *Freedom and Equality,* ed. David Horton. Columbia, Mo., 1960.

White, William S. *The Taft Story.* New York, 1954.

Woodward, C. Vann. *The Strange Career of Jim Crow.* New York, 1966.*

THE COLD WAR

Byrnes, James. *All in One Lifetime.* New York, 1958.

Carr, Albert. *Truman, Stalin and Peace.* New York, 1950.

Clay, Lucius. *Decision in Germany.* New York, 1950.

Davison, W. Phillips. *The Berlin Blockade.* Princeton, 1958.

Deutscher, Issac. *The Great Contest: Russia and the West.* New York, 1960.

Fleming, D.F. *The Cold War and Its Origins,* 1917-1960. 2 vols. N.Y., 1960.

Forrestal, James. *The Forrestal Diaries,* ed. Walter Millis, New York, 1955.

Graebner, Norman. *The New Isolationism.* New York, 1956.

Horowitz, David. *The Free World Colossus.* New York, 1965.*

Hoskins, Halford. *The Atlantic Pact.* Washington, D.C., 1949.

Houghton, Neal D., ed. *Struggle Against History: United States Foreign Policy in an Age of Revolution.* New York, 1960.

Ingram, Kenneth. *History of the Cold War.* New York, 1955.

Kennan, George F. *American Diplomacy,* 1900-1950. Chicago, 1951.*

Kennan, George F. *Russia, The Atom and the West.* New York, 1957.*

LeFeber, Walter, *America, Russia, and the Cold War,* New York, 1968*

Lilienthal, David. *Journals of David Lilienthal,* Vol. II. New York, 1964.

Morgenthau, Hans. *The Impasse of American Foreign Policy,* Chicago, 1962.

Neal, Fred W. *United States Foreign Policy and the Soviet Union.* Santa Barbara, 1961.

Price, Harry. *The Marshall Plan and its Meaning.* Ithaca, 1955.

Schuman, Frederic. *The Cold War: Retrospect and Prospect.* Baton Rouge, 1962.

Stalin, Joseph. *Stalin's Correspondence with Churchill, Attlee, Roosevelt and Truman, 1941-45.* Moscow, 1957.

Williams, William A. *American Russian Relations, 1781-1947.* New York, 1952.

——————————*The Tragedy of American Diplomacy.* New York, 1962.

CHINA POLICY

Beloff, Max. *Soviet Policy in the Far East,* London, 1953.

Fairbank, John K. *The United States and China.* Cambridge, Mass., 1958*

Feis, Herbert. *The China Triangle.* Princeton, 1953.

Westerfield, H. Bradford. *Foreign Policy and Party Politics.* New Haven, 1955.

LOYALTY AND SECURITY

Anderson, Jack, and May, R.W. *McCarthy.* Boston, 1952.

Brown, Ralph. *Loyalty and Security.* New Haven, 1958.

Carr, Robert. *The House Committee on Un-American Activities, 1945-1950.* Ithaca, 1952.

Chambers, Whittaker. *Witness.* New York, 1956.*

Ernst, Morris and Loth, David. *Report on the American Communist.* New York, 1952.

Jowitt, Earl. *The Strange Case of Alger Hiss.* New York, 1953.

McWilliams, Carey. *Witch Hunt: The Revival of Heresy.* Boston, 1950.

Rovere, Richard. *Senator Joe McCarthy.* New York, 1959.

Schlesinger, Arthur, Jr. *The Vital Center.* Cambridge, Mass., 1949.*

Toledano, Ralph de, and Lasky, Victor. *Seeds of Treason: The True Story of the Hiss-Chambers Tragedy.* New York, 1950.

THE KOREAN WAR

Berger, Carl. *The Korean Knot.* Philadelphia, 1964.

Leckie, Robert. *Conflict: The History of the Korean War, 1950-53.* New York, 1962.

MacArthur, Douglas. *Reminiscences.* New York, 1964.

Neustadt, Richard. *Presidential Power: The Politics of Leadership.* New York, 1960.

Rees, David. *Korea: The Limited War.* New York, 1964.

Rovere, Richard and Schlesinger, Arthur Jr. *The General and the President.* New York, 1950.

ESSAYS AND SCHOLARLY ARTICLES

There are literally hundrès of articles available which discuss the Truman administration, its problems, policies, and difficulties. What follows is a brief sampling.

Ader, William. "Why the Dixiecrats Failed," *Journal of Politics, August* 1953.

Bernstein, Barton. "The Truman Administration and Its Reconversion Wage Policy," *Labor History,* Fall, 1965.

——————————"The Truman Administration and the Steel Strike of 1946," *Journal of American History,* March, 1966.

Borchard, Edwin M. "Intervention: The Truman Doctrine and the Marshall Plan," *American Journal of International Law,* Summer, 1947.

Lee, R. Alton. "The Turnip Session of the Do-Nothing Congress: Presidential Campaign Strategy," *Southwestern Social Science Quarterly, December, 1963.*

Lynd, Staughton. "How the Cold War Began," *Commentary,* November, 1960.

Schilling, Warner. "The H-Bomb Decision: How to Decide Without Actually Choosing," *Political Science Quarterly,* March, 1961.

NAME INDEX

154

Nimitz, Chester W., 38
Nixon, Richard M., 43

Patterson, Robert P., 15, 24
Patterson, Roscoe, 6
Paul 1, King of Greece, 47
Pendergast, Michael, 3
Pendergast, Thomas, 3, 5, 6, 8, 11
Perkins, Frances, 13
Pine, David, 42

Rayburn, Sam, 47
Ridgeway, Matthew B., 39
Roosevelt, Eleanor, 12, 47
Roosevelt, Franklin D., 7, 8, 10, 11, 12, 23
Rosenberg, Ethel, 39
Rosenberg, Julius, 39
Royall, Kenneth C., 24
Rummel, Henry, 6

Sawyer, Charles, 28, 42
Schwellenbach, Lewis, 13
Shek, Chiang Kai, 16, 21, 33, 34
Smith, Walter Bedell, 30
Snyder, John W., 20
Sovers, Sidney W., 18
Sparkman, John J., 43
Spottswood, J. J., 48
Stalin, Joseph, 14, 15, 19, 21
Stark, Lloyd, 8
Stettinius, Edward F., 12, 14
Stevenson, Adlai E., 41, 43

Stimson, Henry L., 12, 15
Stone, Harlan F., 12
Symington, Stuart, 46

Taft, Robert A., 25
Taylor, Glenn H., 29
Thurmond, J. Strom, 29, 31
Tobin, Maurice, 30
Torresola, Griselio, 37
Truman, Elizabeth (Bess) Wallace, wife, 4
Truman, John A., father, 1, 2
Truman, Martha Ellen Young, mother, 1, 23, 26
Truman, Mary Jane, sister, 1
Truman, Vivian, brother, 1

Vandenberg, Arthur H., 28, 31
Vaughn, Harry H., 39
Vinson, Fred, 14, 31

Walker, Frank C., 14
Wallace, Henry, 10, 11, 22, 27, 29, 31
Wallgren, Mon, 9
Walter, Francis, 42, 43
Warren, Earl, 29
Wedemeyer, Albert C., 25
Weizmann, Chaim, 26
Wheeler, Burton K., 7, 8
Wickard, Claude R., 13
Wilson, Charles E., 22, 26, 28
Wright, Fielding L., 29

Young, Sol, grandfather, 1

TITLES IN THE OCEANA
PRESIDENTIAL CHRONOLOGY SERIES

Reference books containing Chronology—Documents—Bibliographical Aids for each President covered.

Series Editor: **Howard F. Bremer**

GEORGE WASHINGTON*
edited by Howard F. Bremer

JOHN ADAMS*
edited by Howard F. Bremer

JAMES BUCHANAN*
edited by Irving J. Sloan

GROVER CLEVELAND**
edited by Robert I. Vexler

FRANKLIN PIERCE*
edited by Irving J. Sloan

ULYSSES S. GRANT**
edited by Philip R. Moran

MARTIN VAN BUREN**
edited by Irving J. Sloan

THEODORE ROOSEVELT**
edited by Gilbert Black

BENJAMIN HARRISON*
edited by Harry J. Sievers

JAMES MONROE*
edited by Ian Elliot

WOODROW WILSON**
edited by Robert I. Vexler

RUTHERFORD B. HAYES*
edited by Arthur Bishop

ANDREW JACKSON**
edited by Ronald Shaw

JAMES MADISON*
edited by Ian Elliot

HARRY S TRUMAN***
edited by Howard B. Furer

WARREN HARDING*
edited by Philip Moran

DWIGHT D. EISENHOWER**
edited by Robert I. Vexler

JAMES K. POLK*
edited by John J. Farrell

Available Soon

JOHN QUINCY ADAMS*
edited by Kenneth Jones

HERBERT HOOVER*
edited by Arnold Rice

ABRAHAM LINCOLN**
edited by Ian Elliot

GARFIELD/ARTHUR**
edited by Howard B. Furer

* 96 pages, $3.00/B
** 128 pages, $4.00/B
*** 160 pages, $5.00/B